ALSO BY JUAN GELMAN
TRANSLATED BY LISA ROSE BRADFORD

Oxen Rage

Between Words: Juan Gelman's Public Letter

Commentaries and Citations

Com/positions

PRAISE FOR *TODAY*

Grief and crushing darkness are the inescapable companions of these poems, whose world appears to be as fractured as the grammar and form of Juan Gelman's spare and concentrated verse. In this barbaric place where children are disappeared, where pain never ends and justice is ambivalent, the "poem of harsh lineage" and "unsheltered words" just may find, however, "perfection in the loss." Lisa Rose Bradford translates this difficult news in clean and muscular phrases that push constantly and generatively against the terrible truths of *Today*.

—Sidney Wade

The world of *Today* is the present, a dark forest, that which is here, within and surrounding each of us: the "Today," a strange extreme, unlimited, insistent, inevitable, ungraspable. There are no words to fathom so much reality. Ungraspable, yet inescapable, the present clamours to be named; this is the adventure into which this book hurls itself headlong. The matter is to take charge of *what it is*, as it is, along with the sentiments and commotion that what-it-is unleashes, including the horror, the uncertainty, and the black wall of the void, gaping in the proof of the inevitable. The names of Iraq, Afghanistan, Yemen, and Somalia sidle up to words like NASDAQ, deconstruction, semiotics, God, and symbolic processes. The book speaks of hunger, capitalism, war, and torture, but also of childhood and love, and of poetry, desire, dread, and language. The challenge is to look everything in the eye, without protection or alibies. Seeing what? A world where all explanation falls short, but Gelman refuses to stop asking questions. When there are no answers, one must continue asking questions.

With words failing to clarify this world, these 288 prose poems encircle it with successive broken attempts, a demented and slippery back and forth in order to perhaps touch something, put something into play. Fragments parched and harsh, estranged among themselves, as if the matter now is one of wresting words from the wall of the unsayable, building a poetry that seeks out its own organization, not to transmit what arises, but rather to let words themselves quicken, "Tangents of the tongue continue working in order to ward off sleep."

—Daniel Freidemberg

Juan Gelman's last book is a work that grieves, that savors grief, personal and collective. Or more aptly, as ars poetica, these poems find the impulse to grieve deep in poetry itself—as Gelman has written: "I've never been the owner of my ashes, my poems."

These elegant, chisel's edge inscriptions read like epigrams, like the very first epigrams, which were epitaphs engraved on tombs. The real compression in this poetry—always total—is that "the enormity of the pain covers nothing."

This is a translation that, in its turn, relishes what is lost. Lisa Rose Bradford is remarkably receptive, tuned to the subtlest nuances in Gelman's language, intimate and estranging. This translation is a masterful rendering—and an homage to one of Argentina's greatest poets.

—Michelle Gil-Montero

I find it hard to read *Hoy/Today* without crying, but it's the kind of crying that's good for you. Full of sadness and beauty, spelling out loss and redemption, and absences remembered, the running verses of Juan Gelman's *Hoy* speak of longing, singing with sentiment and love. And Lisa Rose Bradford's version is every bit as compelling as the original reflected in this bilingual edition. There is pain and sorrow here, but also an almost endless source of passion, and compassion. The saving grace, Juan Gelman seems to say to us, is in the beauty and the rhythm of the verses, ringing as true in Lisa Rose Bradford's elegant translations as in Juan Gelman's moving originals. Juan Gelman is an indispensable figure in human rights—and in the tireless and essential labor of love involved in singing through verse.

—Sergio Waisman

This urgent, luminous text is doubly haunted: the poems by the murder of the poet's son, the translations by the death in 2014 of the poet himself. It offers, as Lisa Rose Bradford notes in her fine introduction, "insomniac inventories," flashes of "conflictive beauty," and "extreme condensation of thought and image," as if Gelman were "dragging the canals of thought in order to leave a final testimony." The passion of Gelman's testimony comes through beautifully in Bradford's English.

—Geoffrey Brock

HOY
TODAY

JUAN GELMAN
TRANSLATED BY
LISA ROSE BRADFORD

normal, illinois

Published by co•im•press
Normal, Illinois
www.coimpress.com
co•im•press is a recognized 501(c)(3) nonprofit literary organization.

Printed in the USA by Bookmobile

Distributed to the trade by Small Press Distribution
1341 Seventh Street, Berkeley, CA 94710
www.spdbooks.org

Cover and Book Design by co•im•press
Production Assistant: Sarah Lyons
Cover image: *Blue Tides, Cormorant* by Alice Q. Hargrave, for more
information please visit AliceHargrave.com

Work published within the framework of "Sur" Translation Support
Program of the Ministry of Foreign Affairs and Worship of the
Argentine Republic. Obra editada en el marco del Programa "Sur"
de Apoyo a las Traducciones del Ministerio de Relaciones Exteriores
y Culto de la República Argentina.

First Edition 2018

ISBN: 978-1-947918-00-9

Never did I learn what that rock was
—Sisyphus

Nunca supe qué era esa roca
—Sísifo

POETICS OF UNEASE

"POETRY IS A CURSE, AN OBSESSION," Juan Gelman once told me, "it's a horse that gallops on your chest." In *Hoy/Today*, Gelman's most beautifully compelling and deeply disturbing book of verse, this compulsion is particularly striking, which is no surprise given that its composition was sparked by the sentencing in 2011 of those who murdered his son, Marcelo, whose body was found in a barrel filled with cement in the San Fernando River after he was "detained" in the clandestine Automotores Orletti Center, active during the infamous military dictatorship of Jorge Rafael Videla. Originally entitled "Condenas" (sentences or condemnations), this compendium gathers poems that form different layers of the poet's reflections on the matter: the ceaseless pain of losing a son, the ambivalence of justice, the world's perversity, and the saving graces of passion and beauty in the face of death.

Conjoining the richest qualities of the poetics established in his twenty-plus books of verse, these musings are full of paradox and music and shards of extraordinary imagery, producing an edgy read, a poetics of unease, of "buckskin mares tied round the neck." Scenes from the past, accompanied by thoughts and queries on those visions, are backlit by horror, creating disquieting shapes in the caves of sleepless nights and poetry. Replete with pain and violence, many lines are unsettling if not revolting: "tongue trapped in doorframes"; "Loss broils organs in broad daylight";

"bones beneath a painful downpour." This last line is acutely characteristic of Gelman's disquieting blend of anguish and musicality, which permeates the book: "The marrow of the fallen feeds the rumors of a rose"; "lead-gray leaves drop from the fiasco of their fall"; "The moon travels on waters that move from the heart to midnights of the winched, immobile in another winding down." And the search for the bodies of the disappeared in rivers and unidentified mass graves hovers throughout: "The executed show their holes gorged with patience, moving in bottles still crossing seas"; "Shots in the chest are forever young, free of shame, mists that rained." The paradox of the dead "forever young" and so many other puzzling lines pepper the collection: "in hand an artless rose that knows how not to know"; "absences that do not depart"; "the past yet to come." In fact, a number of the throbbing mysteries seem impossible to decipher, but the enrapturing music of the verse carries us along.

Various poems tend toward insomniac inventories of reckoning, which reflect a rawness, an uncurried surge to get it all down—"When I have fears that I may cease to be / Before my pen has gleaned my teeming brain," as Keats put it—and at 83 years of age, Gelman seemed to be dragging the canals of thought in order to leave a final testimony, perhaps because he sensed a sort of ending since the event of his son's execution had come full circle in legal terms. Flashes from the thirty-five-year struggle to find justice for those killed in the "dirty war" float like jetsam in the verse: exile, gunshots, deaths, hospitals, and identifications ("scrutinized saliva"). Even after the return to democracy in 1983, Gelman was loath to return to Argentina, imagining that he might be walking along the streets of Buenos Aires and have his son's murderers walk right past him. In 2000 his granddaughter, Macarena, was located living with a Uruguayan family—Marcelo's wife, Nora, had given birth while in captivity before her execution—and the author became the sometimes reluctant face of international court battles to find justice for all the families who lost sons and daughters, brothers and sisters, nieces and nephews and, especially, driven by the "Abuelas de Plaza de Mayo" (the Grandmothers of Plaza de Mayo), the grandchildren born in covert centers and given away in adoption during the "Proceso."

Gelman's political activities began at an early age. Son of exiled Ukrainian Jews, he had become a member of the Communist Party in the '50s but soon rejected the party's platforms, principally for reasons of artistic freedom. After spending time in Cuba, he actively participated in the movements that brought back Perón in 1973—both the FAR (Revolutionary Armed Forces) and the guerrilla group Montoneros—and he was subsequently sent to Europe as a journalist in 1975 to work in public relations in the Inter Press of Rome. Condemned by the military coup of 1976, he had to remain in exile in Europe, living mostly in Italy and Spain, finally settling in Mexico. While Gelman continued to denounce human rights abuses, as those same leftist organizations began planning counterattacks from Europe and Mexico during the late '70s, he became more skeptical regarding the leadership and outcome of such schemes and thus disassociated himself from them, but not from the ideals of social justice, which find voice both in essays and poetry.

Even as the revolutionary programs waned, the horse atop his chest never tired, and though he sometimes questioned the role of poetry, he was unable to halt the "galloping" words. As a motif and as a personal memory, the figure of the horse pervades all of Gelman's verse, and this collection is no exception. Words associated with horses—broncos, bits, tack, pasterns—appear throughout. "Beautiful that beloved horse, his legs of cantering off. Kessel watched the twilights with eyes deeper than his wound." His affinity with horses was marked by "el Kessel": as a member of the cavalry, the author was in charge of this parade animal, which the regiment also used on a horse mill for stamping clay to make bricks. When Kessel broke a leg, he was put down and buried, but the next day, as Gelman told the tale, the corpse was gone. "There was a settlement nearby…" he concluded, insinuating a possible answer to the mystery of the missing corpse: "In the foothills shreds of nature settle, horses disappear in a single night / screams and clubbings cannot restore their canter." The splendor of this horse, with his dual purpose and unfortunate but cyclical end, is emblematic of Gelman's way of interlacing the wonder of life and beauty and the torment of hunger and injustice in this world, a reality so often portrayed in his works. Some of these equine figurations are evocative of brute power or the potential of revolution, while others allude to the inspiration to write poetry; in both cases the horse's presence is a mode of bridling memory and conflict.

Horses do not constitute the only personal motif in Gelman's works; a preponderance of birds—symbols of beauty and musicality—can be found from the very inception of his writing—"A bird lived in me. / A flower traversed by blood. / My heart was a violin" (*Violín y otras cuestiones*, 1956). However, in *Today* they embody an element of looming death and corruption: "The skylark didn't want them to dirty her / she said the end / the end." These birds are frightened, beakless, cozened, and deforested: "Hummingbird that departs into dry leaves and a darkened me." Turtledoves, mockingbirds, goldfinches, also appear, often portrayed as sullied or slumbering.

Other tropes of conflictive beauty also arise, especially in the form of roses: "a rose sustains the world," as "strange," "artless," "genuine," "pure," "potential," "sickly," (quoting Blake), "rising up beneath the knives of the moon." Emerging as another motif for splendor, they elicit the question of whether the beauty of the outer world can counterbalance its wretchedness. This ever-present qualm is, moreover, repeatedly figured in the word "fuga," a pun that denotes both escape and fugue, the latter perhaps pointing to a psychological escape through the musicality of poetry: "The vassalage of causalities cinches knots that bind the bond itself. They resist flowers / carnations / roses / flight-bound fugues of transcendence." Indeed, the muse of poetry and song, often invoked as "señora" (in my versions, "my dear"), represents another constant presence in Gelman's work, but she can take the shape of music, or a lover, or his mother, or the motherland, Argentina, country he always returns to in his mind: the Pampas, the horses, the *arrabal* (fringe neighborhoods of tangos and milongas), the plazas and parks of former days of passion.

The concept of passion, or lack thereof, our mode of being in the world and interacting with reality, appears in nearly half of these poems, expressed with the words "passion," "dispassion," "compassion," and in the term "*estar*," (to be). This last word, in contrast with "*ser*" (also, to be), conveys an idea of transience, anticipating either a gerund or a complementary adjective, so to be used alone creates a disconcerting strangeness in the text, perhaps suggesting a "being-here-now." "El ser / estar / unidos en distancias ontológicas" ("To be / to be here / joined in ontological distances") begins one illustrative poem, which underscores a distance between modes of being and being-here now—with presence and passion—in an antithesis of presence and absence or beginnings and endings.

Encapsulated within non-lineated blocks, these captivating texts might be classified as prose poems, particularly in light of Baudelaire's "dream of the miracle of a poetic prose, music without rhyme, supple and muscular enough to accommodate the lyrical movement of the soul, the undulations of reverie, the bump and lurch of consciousness." These sonorous meditations are nothing if not supple and muscular, and the extreme condensation of thought and image takes the verse to the very edge with paratactic gaps and puzzling appositions that resist both reading and translation. Though they seem to flow toward narrative or scene, expectations constantly "bump and lurch" as the slits between sentence and sentence must be sutured by the reader's imagination.

Within these lurching lines, wordplay and musicality are often in sharp contrast with the torturous subject matter of this book, and the translation of this verse must maintain, on the one hand, the encompassing ambiguity of these leaps, and, on the other, the collision of euphonic beauty and agonizing imagery. Gelman, as one postmodern critic once dismissingly quipped, "is, in the end, a lyrical poet." Thus, it is essential that Gelman's poetics of unease be represented with a comparable coupling of sonorous delight and semantic dread.

Each language, however, is like a unique musical instrument, full of its own particular traditions and virtuosity. Spanish, with far fewer sounds is easier to rhyme and tends to use facile internal assonance and consonance marked by rumbling trills that English does not possess. Also, being a highly inflected language, Spanish enjoys great flexibility in syntactic order. The English language must, nevertheless, be played here according to the potential sublimity of its instrument, for example, working with rhythm in monosyllabic words and the subtle chiming of abundant consonant or vowel sounds and bilabial combinations that invite recitation. Thus, I have attempted to recreate an analogous euphony with those English harmonies, leading me, so long as the meaning is not skewed, to form melodic and balanced rhythms and to choose words and phrases of heightened sonority. I have often elected, moreover, to suppress awkward repetitions of pronouns, opting rather for gerunds, commas, or, quirky Gelmanian slashes, even when they are not present in the Spanish versions.

Regarding Gelman's generally idiosyncratic punctuation, the very title of the closing poem of this volume presents a troublesome bind:

¿Y

si la poesía fuera un olvido del perro que te mordió
la sangre / una delicia falsa / una fuga en mí mayor
/ un invento de lo que nunca se podrá decir? ¿Y si
fuera la negación de la calle / la bosta de un caballo
/ el suicidio de los ojos agudos? ¿Y si fuera lo que es
un cualquier parte y nunca avisa? ¿Y si fuera?

Odd in Spanish with this indeterminate punctuation—a question opens with an inverted question mark and then closes with a normal one to ensure the proper tenor—this mark leads the reader to ask where this question ends, making the title either an open-ended query or an unstable part of the body of the poem. How can this be achieved in English? With "What if"; "And?"; or by brazenly including an inverted question mark, expanding the English language to suggest the proper Adornean "tonality"? As questions are central to Gelman's poetics and thus deserve to be particularly visible in translation, and since this final poem depends so awfully on this questioning tone, after great deliberation, I decided to include the unorthodox usage of an inverted mark in the English version:

¿And

if poetry were a forgotten memory of the dog that
mauled your blood / a false delight / a fleeting fugue
in the time-worn key of me / an invention of what
can never be said? And if it were the denial of the
street / the suicide of two keen eyes / horse manure?
And if it were just some anywhere that never sends
word? And if it were?

Punctuation is not the only translational challenge in this poem: the puns are terribly perplexing: again, *fuga* (escape and/or fugue) and *mi mayor* (E major and/or older me). In the same initial line, the repetition of /p/ and /r/ in the Spanish find their musical English patterning in the /d/ and /ô/, "forgotten," "memory," "dog," "mauled," "blood," which underscores the clash between form and topic. In short, matters of ambiguity and sound in *Today* are harrowing as they are exhilarating for the translator.

The final line of this poem with its subjunctive mood, "if it were," anticipates a noun or complementary adjective, rather like Hamlet's "to be," thus ending the volume, published just months before the poet's passing, with an intriguing uncertainty—and if poetry were... useful? revolutionary? "lasting"?—reinstating the double-edged doubt of being or being-here and not being. Is poetry "worth the while" (the title of one of his collections) or just "horse manure," or is it both? Gelman mulls the place of poetry and the need to act, especially in the face of past errors and debatable justice; however, "To be sure," he once wrote to me, "is the sickness of our times." In the face of absence and incertitude, one must generate beauty by being present and passionate.

Juan Gelman's mode of marrying splendor and pain through the exploration of the tongue's potential within a montage of delirious images and paradoxical notions sets the past and present cantering into the mind of the reader. But the question lingers: can verse invent "what can never be said"? Gelman never flinched. Keeping his head close to the pasterns of "the horse that gallops best," he generated poems of passion, which he gifted to friends in his numerous dedications and offered to his readers with the finely crafted music and melancholy of these resonant meditations on the day.

Lisa Rose Bradford
Mar del Plata, Argentina
December 2017

HY
TODAY

|

Life departing leaves an airy murmur in the core of a hand
that is senseless to kiss. Treat it well, my dear, do not misjudge
the dishes you have warmed and served, dreams, overcoats,
obscurities, clarity, refrains of the faith, pain in the middle of
the day, things of beauty that should always remain.

|

La vida que se va deja un soplo en medio de la mano que
es inútil besar. Trátelo bien, señora, no equivoque los platos
que calentó y sirvió, sueños, abrigos, oscuridades, claridad,
la fe que se repite, dolores en la mitad del día, bellezas que
se deben quedar.

||

Do not touch my solitude / a nightless dog / time lying low / fallow land. Institutions of mercy seal their lips, no one shatters the pane where I watch you play what you dreamt so hard one day. I listen in bits and pieces.

||

No me toquen la soledad / perro sin noche / tiempo que se abajó / baldíos. Los organismos de la piedad cierran la boca, nadie raja el cristal donde te veo tocar lo que soñabas tanto un día. Escucho a pedacitos.

||||

God has flown off to the void left by his death. Shadows swallow up the landfalls and love's favors are dumped on sundry streets. Life resembled life once upon a time / not even lies fly now. Such a filthy state, the world must be swept clean / once again serpent eggs are laid / so ancient.

||||

Dios se fue al vacío que dejó su muerte. La sombra traga los regresos y los favores del amor en cualquier calle se abandonan. La vida se pareció a la vida alguna vez / ya la mentira ni siquiera vuela. Hay que barrer el mundo en sucio estado / otra vez ponen huevos de serpiente / viejos.

IV

Dearth builds inhabited worlds / fables of rendezvous / depositions of passion. Desire does not long for death when confronted with the corpse of desire. The I turns toward an ungraspable you / sidesteps the shorter days / that which wrests heart from heart. The was of being-here now bursts in on night / heads for the core of the closed eyelid. Experience has no conscience / it drifts in its talents like a wealthy beggar.

For José Ángel Leyva

IV

La carencia construye mundos habitados / fábulas del encuentro / constancias del ardor. El deseo no se quiere morir ante el cadáver del deseo. El yo se dirige a un vos incomprensible / elude los días cortos / lo que saca corazón del corazón. El fue de estar interrumpe la noche / va al centro del párpado cerrado. La experiencia no tiene conciencia / vaga en sus atributos como un mendigo rico.

A José Ángel Leyva

∬

Prometheus never revealed how to steal fire / how death from the dead / how hands from receiving their nothing. Limits drown in their limits and no one lends them a handkerchief so once and for all they might have a good cry.

∬

Prometeo nunca dijo cómo se roba el fuego / cómo la muerte al muerto / cómo las manos a recibir su nada. Los límites se ahogan en sus límites y nadie les da un pañuelo para que lloren de una buena vez.

VI

Desire is and so as to be, is not. We are what we are not between dark sheets. Blind horses graze on the plains of the tongue, gallop in their out-of-kilter breadth, hope for nothing more than nothingness, the only space where pairing is possible.

VI

El deseo es y para ser, no es. Somos lo que no somos en sábanas oscuras. La llanura de la lengua tiene caballos ciegos, galopan su dimensión qualunque sin otra esperanza que la nada, el único lugar donde la unión es posible.

VII

In pondering death, death becomes transformed. From reason to delirium there's a journey / passengers galore / constant roadblocks / stations. Bulls horses, names boggled in violence. The equivocal face of error never adorned the caves. Being here is a naked task. Unease and the self with nowhere to moor.

VII

Pensar la muerte cambia a la muerte. De razón a delirio hay un viaje / muchos pasajeros / clausuras constantes / estaciones. Los toros los caballos, nombres por violencia asombrada. Nadie pintó en las cavernas el rostro incierto de la equivocación. Estar es un trabajo desnudo. La desazón de sí no tiene puerto.

VIII

How much blood does it take / to travel from knowing to contradiction / from forgetting to horror / from injustice to justice? Must one touch the burning altars / evade the shame / the absence that harrowed Theognis / the day's interruption? The desire for ties becomes a noose pulled tight by the killer. A limitless, bottomless, worthless detour. Selfhood is a broken mirror in the third person and I can hear your hand sketching a lazuline bird.

For Marcelo

VIII

¿Cuánta sangre cuesta / ir de saber a la contradicción / del olvido al horror / de la injusticia a la justicia? ¿Hay que tocar los altares ardientes / evitar la vergüenza / la falta que preocupaba a Teognis / interrupción del día? El deseo del lazo se convierte en el lazo que el asesino ajusta. Desvío sin límite ni fondo ni virtud. La mismidad es un espejo roto en tercera persona y oigo tu mano dibujando un pájaro azul.

A Marcelo

IX

The exile of delight, the unruly powers of the spirit, mirrors of invented philosophy. Well-spent the life given for a canary's trill with fresh perfume and nary a soul to sully it.

IX

El exilio del goce, las potencias sin orden del espíritu, espejos de la filosofía inventada. Vale la pena dar la vida por un gorjeo de canario con fresco olor y nadie que lo ensucie.

X

Eternity is such a violent notion / capitalist / the accumulation of future. Whirling its light in the breath of dew, consciousness is freed from itself. The blaze of pillows where time walks naked, and love's order is lost. Night ripens / the body's truths become acquainted with the wooing retinue / the hours that slip away.

X

La eternidad es una idea violenta / capitalista / acumular futuro. La conciencia se libra de sí misma cuando vira su luz en las respiraciones del rocío. Fulgor de las almohadas en las que el tiempo se desnuda y el orden del amor se pierde. La noche madura / las verdades del cuerpo conocen el cortejo / las horas que se van.

XI

They give back the ruins of innocence, pebbles in the breeze, oceanless anchors, birdless woods. Gatherings that once had a voice / devastated / the tongue's vacillations. Incessant the boroughs cyclone against the era's exterminations, feet sunk in endless cruelty, its savage batons. The languor of love toils away still, painting eyes yet without flight. Dawn sings adrift on ferocious nights. Cowards put fears to bed in the natural shock of disaster. They have no idea how to take it underwing.

XI

Devuelven ruinas de inocencia, piedras en la brisa, anclas sin mar, bosques sin aves. Encuentros que tuvieron voz / devastados / vacilaciones de la lengua. El barrio no cesa su ciclón contra exterminios de la época, pies hundidos en la crueldad sin término, sus bastones salvajes. Las lentitudes del amor labran y pintan ojos sin alas todavía. El alba canta sin camino en noches fieras. Los cobardes acuestan miedos en las crepitaciones del desastre. No lo saben cuidar.

XII

Chiaroscuro murdered the light / night drags on / dense.
When I enter the room I never enter, the accident bobs up.
A law of its own creation. Madly it laughs at the man intent
on pumping blood to his mill. The sails are set spinning at
the mere sight of a rose-bellied bunting. Fine perception
ebbs in the noxious prison of what we're not / lead-gray
leaves drop from the fiasco of their fall.

XII

El claroscuro mató a la luz / la noche dura / tanto. Cuando
entro en la habitación que nunca entro, el accidente flota.
Es una ley de su creación. Se ríe locamente del fijado en
llevar sangre a su molino. Giran las aspas al menor paseo
de un colorín azul. La percepción sensible se intoxica en la
cárcel de lo que no somos / caen hojas grises de su otoño
fallido.

XIII

Noises of everyday death reach our ears / Mexico / Iraq /
Pakistan / Afghanistan / Yemen / Somalia. At a loss I look
at myself / I'm the assassin and the assassinated. Farewell,
candor, the remnants of childhood grow wan / no food
left to give them. The beauty of a sleeping bird leaves me
in agony and I beg the bird go back to sleep. No trees of
corporeal loveliness, no lengthy days of May.

XIII

Llegan los ruidos de la muerte cotidiana / México / Irak
/ Pakistán / Afganistán / Yemen / Somalia. Me miro sin
explicaciones / soy el asesino y el asesinado. Adiós, candor,
los restos de la infancia están pálidos / no hay qué darles de
comer. La belleza de un pájaro dormido me trae agonías
y ruego al pájaro que duerma. Sin árboles de hermosura
corpórea, sin largos días de mayo.

XIV

The fair's penitentiary has neither *diamond doors nor golden bolts. Sorrow, hunger, war, infamy, sadness, even death* / all stroll by at wing's length with the plummeting linnet. Hate you've forgotten, and resignation and ire, Balthazar. The thoroughfares cool in the disciplines of humiliation and no healthy breezes blow, feasible contracts for common ground between spiritual fears and the hues of a heron. Dignity intones a gaunt melody / sandy eyelids / clamping shut its source of blood. Indignation forgets its blaze. Life, what are they doing to you, there all alone, homeless, in need of parables, in the evaporation of each and every dream.

For Tomás Segovia

XIV

La cárcel de la feria *no tiene puertas de diamante ni candados de oro. La pena, el hambre, la guerra, la infamia, la tristeza, hasta la misma muerte* / se pasean a dedos del jilguero que cae malherido. Te olvidaste del odio, la resignación, la furia, Baltasar. Las disciplinas de la humillación enfrían la vía pública y no soplan vientos de salud, los contratos posibles del encuentro entre los miedos del espíritu y los colores de una garza. La dignidad canta músicas flacas / párpados de arena / le clavan la fuente de la sangre. La indignación olvida sus fulgores. Vida, qué te hacen, vida, sola ahí, sin techo ni parábolas, en la evaporación de cualquier sueño.

A Tomás Segovia

XV

Alchemies sinter the pain. Planets drive nature's wheels / Mercury is a dragon, husband and wife unto itself / fecundating poison that in a single day will slay what is hanging on to life. Does its feminine side slip away like a babe abandoning the womb? Does Neptune nurse the ashes of death in Juarez, Port-au-Prince, Sana, Veracruz? Does the poem of the Sun and the Moon don the disguise of a crownless cloud? The ministers of the eye resume their work with assessable beasts.

XV

El dolor cuece con alquimias. Los planetas empujan las ruedas de la naturaleza / Mercurio es un dragón esposo y esposa de sí mismo / fecunda en un día el veneno que mata lo que aún vive. ¿Su parte femenina se le va como quien abandona su placenta? ¿Neptuno cuida cenizas de la muerte en Ciudad Juárez, Puerto Príncipe, Sana, Veracruz? ¿El poema de la Luna y el Sol se disfraza de nube sin corona? Los ministros del ojo retoman su trabajo con bestias calculables.

XVI

Fear normalizes danger when / the assassin scours the town
street by street / the tongue files away the rest / first woman
stoned to death / incertitude / ideas behind an unnumbered
door. There are voices known to none / a sickle razed them
all. Countries where we were born and where we were not
gather us together with what they always were / cruelty
dangling from dread.

XVI

El temor normaliza el peligro cuando / el asesino recorre
calle a calle / la lengua guarda todo lo que falta / mujer
primera que apedrearon / la incertidumbre / las ideas en un
lugar sin número. Hay voces de las que nadie sabe nada /
una hoz las segó. Patrias en las que nacimos y no nacimos
nos juntan con lo que siempre fueron / crueldad colgada
del pavor.

XVII

They hand you a plate of beauty and poison. Madness fills the edges / the debt for what we are not. With the eyes of a lynx / loathings with no amber to sate them / time transfixed in its passing / violence in its sickly cultivation. With a splash of noble passion and on foot they long to open up the wonder, sought out in the heart of a lotus in the briefest of seasons / with a bullet if need be.

XVII

Sirven un plato con porciones de belleza y veneno. La locura ocupa muchas partes en límites del plato / la deuda con lo que no somos / el tiempo fijo en su pasar / odios sin ámbar que los sacie. Tienen ojos de lince / violencias en su cultivo enfermo. Desean abrir la maravilla a pie, apenas un chorrito de la noble pasión, la que buscaba el blanco de un nenúfar en la estación más breve / a tiros si es preciso.

XVIII

The loss of self in search of self is selfsame love by natural means, groping without understanding, shock's sightlessness. Free of demagogies, solitude has the secret's transparency / rampant benweed / longing's gales. They spit blood when struck a blow and nothing alters their twisted shapes. Black fruit of the shepherd's staff / their forbidden innards must be mulled face to face.

XVIII

La pérdida de uno en su buscarse es mesmo amor por vía natural, tanteos sin entendimiento, ceguera de alarmado. La soledad sin demagogias tiene la transparencia del secreto / malayerbas crecidas / tormentas del deseo. Escupen sangre cuando se las golpea y nada cambia su forma atravesada. Son frutos negros del cayado / hay que mirarles cara a cara las entrañas prohibidas.

XIX

Raymond Roussel found impressions of Africa on the French dairy farm of a rolled-sleeved blonde / there are continents on fire though missing four corners / color's muted actions. A notebook holds thoughts on courage and many empty pages with the slippery gap of times to come. There, love birds perch, original ignorance / a tiny place for what never was / shielded by an eclipse of virgins.

XIX

Raymond Roussel encontró impresiones de África en un tambo francés de rubia arremangada / hay continentes que arden aunque tengan cuatro rincones menos. Son las acciones mudas del color. Una libreta guarda anotaciones del coraje y muchas páginas vacías con la oblicua fisura de tiempos que vendrán. Ahí se estacionan tórtolas, las ignorancias del principio / un pequeño lugar para lo que no fue. Un eclipse de vírgenes lo cuida.

XX

Who said time petrifies tears? They may go into hiding, hold up in dens of delirium. The nothingness of a starving child's skin-bones augments the mires of dread. In the face-off with the photo no one breathes a word. The parity of extremes in sordid seasons creates projects of emptiness, and desolation pretends to be the one who sheds no tears, inscapes tilting out of kilter with no reinvention in sight.

XX

¿Quién dijo que el tiempo petrifica las lágrimas? Se esconderán por ahí, en las moradas del delirio. Los huesos pura piel de un niño muerto de hambre aumentan lodos del espanto. En el careo con la foto nadie habla. La paridad de los extremos en estaciones sórdidas crea proyectos de vacío y la desolación finge ser una que no llora, se ladea el paisaje mental sin reinvención posible.

XXI

One cannot translate the crisis of the Iron Age. The brain's redactions continue with their diagrammatic jackets / encompassing the winters of childhood / the plunders that do not hand themselves over / the tree that bows when they pass by. The world reeks with bad animus and defiles the deep-seated unity of its double. Future times live on in the secret gullet of a finch.

For Pepe Nun

XXI

La crisis de la edad de hierro no tiene traducción. Las escrituras del cerebro siguen con su chaleco diagramático / abarcan inviernos de la niñez / despojos que no renuncian a sí mismos / el árbol que se inclina cuando pasan. El mundo tiene mal aliento y mancha la unidad profunda de la doble. En el buche secreto de un jilguero vive lo que vendrá.

A Pepe Nun

XXII

Capitalism forgot about the party. It can't sit by the fire to banter with you, pelt you with hatred, war, corn or chocolate, the very knots of sin. It blockades all roads from bitter to sweet, anxiety's disappearances, a brusque dream between two moons. It doesn't believe in the desire that perceives its own imperfections. It takes shelter in the gold of others and fashions eternities that are not.

For Paola

XXII

El capitalismo se olvidó de la fiesta. No se sienta frente al fuego para hablarle, tirarle odios, guerras, maíz o chocolate, los nudos del pecado. Prohíbe los caminos de la amargura al dulzor, las desapariciones de la angustia, un sueño brusco entre dos lunas. No cree en el deseo que ve su imperfección. Se ampara en oro ajeno y trabaja eternidades que no existen.

A Paola

XXIII

Infinity kills off non-constituted beings / what rebellion leaves
it infirm? / how long must hope lie hoping? Sentimental waves
are drowning the question how long must hope lie hoping.
Melancholy's physicians write prescriptions / pointless
existing / needs / empty hands / candor's discomfort.

XXIII

El infinito mata seres no constituidos / ¿qué rebelión lo
enferma? / ¿cuánto tiene que esperar la esperanza? Olas
sentimentales ahogan la pregunta cuánto tiene que esperar
la esperanza. Los médicos de la melancolía dan recetas / no
sirven hay / necesidades / manos vacías / desasosiegos del
candor.

XXIV

The hiatus of passion is not covered in ash. There are questions, mother's scoldings, other declensions to name the patios of the past. Muddled tongues traverse every rainfall. The dignities of the void are earthbound creatures, the price for their sacrifice, smoke. A stellar fragment warms the water where we wash our extremes, their illusory challenges. Accounts payable, furniture of the sorrow, disguises for the cartilage. Incertitude reigns and rasps the moon's inversions. You are there and remain mindful of the evanescence of grace. When will you find respite.

XXIV

Los descansos de la pasión no están cubiertos de ceniza. Hay preguntas, regaños de la madre, otras declinaciones para nombrar los patios del pasado. Opacidades de la lengua recorren cada lluvia. Las dignidades del vacío son animales de la tierra y el precio de su sacrificio es humo. Un pedazo estelar calienta el agua donde lavamos nuestro extremo, su reto imaginado. Deudas abiertas, muebles del dolor, disfraces del cartílago. La incertidumbre es reina y raspa las inversiones de la luna. Estás ahí y no olvidás la ligereza de la gracia. Cuándo descansarás.

XXV

The letter's date marks a time of no return. The before and after rivet perplexities of absence, photographs on no one's walls. Impossibility lingers / leadens. It's not the letter's reasons. Its melodious breath holds souls ventilating on a wizened filament of power / simple earnings of being-here now / alive the words that fall silent.

XXV

La fecha de la carta marca un tiempo sin vuelta. El antes y el después clavan perplejidades de la ausencia, fotos en la pared de nadie. La imposibilidad dura / dura. No son razones de la carta. En su respiración canora hay almas ventiladas por un poder delgado / ganancias simples del estar / vivo el decir que calla.

XXVI

Frenzies lie in the underground of experience, rage that locks horns with the onslaught of melancholy. Nature humiliates lordly arrogance, cashing in on equivocal lots in savage banks. The vulgar omen of poverty returns to its post. Someone inquires regarding the infrastructures of horror as if Sor Juana's swans had been unable to unseal that mystery. Ours is a time of inner desertions. The link between things and their naming yields so little, and death rains down from golden clouds.

For Marco Antonio Campos

XXVI

Hay furores en la clandestinidad de la experiencia, iras que embisten los arrimos de la melancolía. La naturaleza humilla a la soberbia señoril, levanta mal su suerte en bancos del salvaje. El presagio común de la miseria vuelve a su posición. Alguien pregunta por infraestructuras del horror como si los cisnes de Sor Juana no pudieran abrir ese misterio. Es el tiempo de las deserciones interiores. La relación entre las cosas y la palabra que las nombra no rinde y nubes de oro llueven muerte.

A Marco Antonio Campos

XXVII

The living traits of the beast are unacquainted with clocks and repose. As if made of motherless steel they chain themselves to ignorance and will not slay one another before taking their leave. Having deforested the hummingbird's virtue, their reason has become a peaking stock. O that Marcabru could return to tell us *what they have made of us, souls cowering on the road, extinguishers of firebrands,* the infamy of the chieftains. The silhouette must be cut in the niches of failure. The mourning soars from its house to its house.

XXVII

Los aspectos vivientes de la bestia no conocen relojes ni descanso. Se engarzan a ignorancias como si fueran hierro sin señora y no se matarán antes de irse. Deforestaron la virtud del colibrí y se cotiza su razón. Que vuelva Marcabrú a decirnos *cómo nos hicieron, apagadores del tizón, los agachados del camino,* la infamia de los jefes. Hay que cortarse la silueta en los rincones del fracaso. El duelo vuela de su casa a su casa.

XXVIII

Compassion holds the deeds to barren lots, they need kidnapping / torture / murder / to be words without matter, distracted / retreating / dislodged from military dictatorships / from living bodies hurled into oceans. The tenants of deafness / before / after / hawking oblique longing, black deserts, escape. And what to do with other-words / capitalism's savagery / children dying before their childing? / *Do you know your knowledge, child?* Benn would ask. To bear the cruelest climes / they deliver light when they can / whelp animals dressed as civilians as if that were such a big deal.

XXVIII

La compasión tiene lotes estériles, necesitan que secuestro / tortura / asesinato / sean palabras sin material, distraídas / retrocedentes / no pegadas a dictadura militar / a cuerpos vivos tirados al océano. Los inquilinos del no oír / antes / después / mercadean ansias oblicuas, desiertos negros, fugas. ¿Y qué hacer con las palabras otras / salvajerías del capitalismo / niños que mueren antes de su niño? / *¿Sabés tu saber, niño?* preguntaba Benn. Soportar las estaciones crudas / alumbran cuando pueden / dan animales vestidos de civil como si fuera tanto.

XXIX

You thought a hawk was not allowed on the beloved cheek,
nor broken goblets worth the while. Faces you gave with no
more love than love now navigate the shards of fate. Soon
they'll be searching, eyes shut tight, for some dolphin in
your bay.

For Jorge Boccanera

XXIX

Pensaste que un halcón no es permisible en la mejilla amada
ni valen copas rotas. En los pedazos de la suerte navegan
rostros que diste sin más querer que querer. Ya buscarán con
párpados cerrados algún delfín en tu bahía.

A Jorge Bocccanera

XXX

The despot of disappearances awards the country where the bullets are these. The soul resorts to meetings with others / the good / the bad. The avocado lends a splash of green to the musical confessions / each note a lie. Concealed in what is banned is the right to wailing's angry battles. The injuries of others mate with one's own as agony spits and sputters on the fire. The enormity of the pain covers nothing. See it there, changing flowers, flights, the mother's table / copper forks and spoons from the Black Sea. What came before now measures the desires of the days and of the nights on a clock with no hands.

XXX

El caudillo de las desapariciones premia al país donde los balazos son éstos. El alma acude a su reunión con los otros / los del bien / los del mal. El aguacate le da verde a confesiones musicales / mienten cada nota. Lo que se esconde en lo vedado es el derecho a las batallas furiosas del gemido. El daño ajeno toca al propio con sus chisporroteos de calvario. El tamaño del dolor no cubre nada. Ahí se lo ve, cambiando flores, vuelos, la mesa de la madre / los cubiertos de cobre del Mar Negro. Lo que fue mide el deseo de la noche y el deseo del día con un reloj que anda mal.

XXXI

Summer sweeps up the remnants of explanations and burns them in innocence. Victims and executioners gather in an excruciating corner. In the perplexities of a planet swept away by the hour, each moment is a chasm that hisses I cannot sanction the evil / tongue trapped in doorframes. The loss is a waking dream. There are tobacco leaves with the smoky conceit of delay, scarecrows for fathers, the stand-ins for Death that hardly know him.

XXXI

El verano recoge restos de explicaciones y los quema con candor. Víctimas y verdugos se juntan en un rincón insoportable. En las perplejidades de un planeta borrado por la hora cada momento es un aujero con silbos de no acepto el mal / lengua atrapada en filos de la puerta. Su pérdida es un soñar despierto. Hay hojas de tabaco con humos del retraso, espantapájaros de padre, reemplazos de la muerte que la conocen mal.

XXXII

Does nature proscribe every remedy for your loss? Shall I postpone your burial, though I carried what was left of you to my parents' resting place? Your shadow keeps a vigil over clockless messages. Memory has meadows where you always graze and diapers I don't know how to change. The hardest link joins you to the one who visits and he is crux and fixed.

XXXII

¿La naturaleza expulsa cualquier remedio de tu pérdida? ¿Aplazo el acto de enterrarte, aunque llevé lo que de vos quedaba junto al descanso de mis padres? Tu sombra cuida mensajes sin reloj. La memoria tiene pastos que siempre te comés y pañales que no sé cambiar. El eslabón más duro te une al que te visita y está cruz y fijado.

XXXIII

Mourning's paths elude the fulfilment of duty, their cunning lets them survive / countries / lairs of being-here now. The impossibility of erasing all traces anchors itself in what is real with unstoppable pendulums / its similitude to death is scandalous.

XXXIII

Los caminos del duelo eluden el deber cumplido, tienen audacias para sobrevivir / países / escondrijos de estar. La imposibilidad de borrar huellas ancla en el real con péndulos indetenibles / su semejanza con la muerte es un escándalo.

XXXIV

In the diagrams of cruelty there's a dog digging for its pardon. Mountainous shams of goodness lie in capitalism's molars / biting / chewing / grinding / ingesting the day that was worth a hundred. Where now is the thief that stole his own self to be granted space for a bogus life? Thoughts in want of human radiance dance to the fugue of flight / deaf / blind / not wanting the sightless to find their eyes. The struggle is standing in the corner. Roving swallows lay eggs amid the bodies of the drought. Lonely births prevail, set in motion by a man who is songless on nights that seem to fly right by.

For Alberto Szpunberg

XXXIV

En los diagramas del maltrato un perro cava su perdón. Hay montañas de bondad fingida en los molares del capitalismo / muerden / mascan / comen / trituran del día que valió por cien. ¿Dónde quedó el ladrón de sí para darle lugar a vida falsa? Los pensamientos sin fulgor humano bailan las danzas de la fuga / no oyen / no ven / no quieren el encuentro de un ciego con sus ojos. La lucha está de cara a su rincón. Las golondrinas ambulantes ponen huevos entre los cuerpos de la seca. Hay nacimientos solos y los va a inaugurar el que no canta en noches que le duran poco.

A Alberto Szpunberg

XXXV

So, bits of me, call an assembly and decide. Don white
hats and red suspenders, a dash of color so the old ox can
hit the road. My dead are casting shadows, hopeless cases
now. They sink their boartusks in, my dear, frozen kisses in
depiction of autumns past, vessels searching for a sea.

XXXV

A ver, pedazos míos, hagan asamblea y decidan. Pónganse
sombreros blancos y tiradores rojos, haya color para que el
viejo buey se vaya. Mis muertos ponen sombras porque no
tienen más remedio. Clavan dientes de jabalí, señora, besos
helados en representación de otoños idos, naves que buscan
algún mar.

XXXVI

Ferocious faces stand agape when love becomes acquainted with the instruments of its death. The word's every corner becomes diffused into incertitudes, shoreless oceans, treading on the transparency of a diamond. Unquavering, reason raises steel, ignorant of bygone joys. A bird nibbles away at the acacia's song, its flight constrained in fixed contents, no doors, no exit. Fury is born of itself / the linden trees recall two youths / strolling on nights that grew soft / amid the gunshots of the times. Today they continue to stroll as shadows and do not say why.

XXXVI

Se abren rostros feroces cuando el amor conoce los instrumentos de su muerte. Rincones de la palabra se desbaratan en incertidumbres, mares sin playa, pisan la transparencia de un diamante. La razón levanta fierros sin temblor, analfabeta de la dicha que hubo. Un ave come el canto de una acacia y vuela en contenidos fijos sin puerta ni salida. La furia nace sola / recuerdan a dos jóvenes los tilos / sus paseos en noches que volvían suaves / entre balazos de la época. Pasean hoy mismo como sombras y no dicen por qué.

XXXVII

Eyes lurk in the order of the broken mirror. The alternative movement of glorious sentiments stumbles like a lame man fighting a losing battle / compassion aroused / doubts of the ancient troubadour. Where are the friends of the danger to come / to change it all? Who is wagering unsung gashes for one cantering joy? Seen and measured bit by bit / midway between desire and its speech / one returns to prior times / to what is coming / defeat purchased by the silence of a sylvan nightingale.

XXXVII

Hay ojos en el orden del espejo roto. El movimiento alternativo de sentimientos célebres tropieza como rengo en batallas perdidas / lástimas despiertas / dudas de trovador antiguo. ¿A dónde fueron amistades del peligro a venir / cambiar todo? ¿Quién se juega desgarros sin canción por una dicha a galopar? Visto y medido pedazo por pedazo / medio camino entre el deseo y su discurso / se vuelve a lo anterior / a lo que viene / la derrota pagada por el silencio de un ruiseñor silvestre.

XXXVIII

Between the active and the passive organ, pity is born, sprouting from sudden hate like some senseless vine. It stretches the limits of lycanthropy, memory takes stock of its zoo and no one knows who is night anymore. It changes loss into blameless diamonds. Does the experience of the void enter Eden with no before / sorrow / works / broken bonds / sweat? Does death grow weary in its wrinkles? Do monsters lurk in the riverbeds of motionless repose?

For Geneviève Fabry

XXXVIII

Entre el órgano activo y el pasivo sucede la piedad. Nace del odio de repente como una enredadera sin razón. Alarga límites de la licantropía, la memoria recorre su zoológico y no se sabe más quién es la noche. Convierte lo perdido en diamantes sin culpa. ¿Las experiencias del abismo entran en el edén sin antes / penas / trabajos / lazos rotos / sudor? ¿La muerte se fatiga arrugada? ¿En el reposo de lo inmóvil hay monstruos bajo el río?

A Geneviève Fabry

XXXIX

What ends without ever having begun is a smothered flower that reopens its petals without song. The bulk of time walks by without seeing or touching it. The theoreticians of romantic combat possess virtues fretted by logic / sporadic / they go from the trembling twig in the beak of a bird to tossing out all their ghosts. Loss stands in admiration of the will behind what never was, drowning more than one heavenly body in its arid combinations. These are the roads lent to the ill at ease between earth and a cosmos that one day will come to an end.

For Jean Allouch

XXXIX

Lo que termina sin empezar es una flor que se apagó y reabre sus pétalos sin canto. El tamaño del tiempo pasa a su lado sin mirar, ni la toca. Los teóricos del duelo romántico tienen virtudes comidas por la lógica / alternan / pasan de la rama que tiembla en el pico de un pájaro a echar a la basura sus fantasmas. La pérdida admira esa voluntad del nunca fue, ahoga a más de un astro en sus combinaciones secas. Son caminos prestados al incómodo de sí entre la tierra y el cosmos que cierto día finirá.

A Jean Allouch

XL

A state's progenies / Power gnaws at their changes / reducing them to smaller mien. Where are the poplars that demanded their space in order to offer shade? Cores of more to less / shores at rest / something with the sheen of truth. The disappearances have thirst glands / the masks of Eros / world without vineyards / accidents / so much is left behind, irreparable.

XL

Las crías de un estado / el Poder les come la mudanza / las convierte en apariencia chica. ¿Dónde quedaron álamos que reclamaban su lugar para dar sombra? Núcleos de más a menos / orillas en reposo / algo que se parezca a la verdad. Las desapariciones tienen glándulas de sed / máscaras de Eros / mundo sin viñas / accidentes / tanto se queda atrás y sin remedio.

XLI

The speeches' gaps will seed never-ending fires. The child cleft of children / the song trimmed by eccentric scissors / the progression of cruelty at a thousand miles per dollar / names of passion with no dictionary. The choirs of the void see themselves in the voiceless man with his hand poised on the edge. The opposite side of the spell is one solid piece / piloted by gunshots that may come.

XLI

Todo lo que no existe en los discursos siembra fuegos que no terminan más. El niño mutilado de los niños / el canto recortado por extrañas tijeras / la progresión de la crueldad a mil kilómetros por dólar / nombres de la pasión sin diccionario. Los coros del vacío se reconocen en el mudo con una mano en el confín. El revés del conjuro es de una sola pieza y lo navegan tiros que vengan.

XLII

Those who kiss cast stones at their monsters. The task of killing death fits inside a tiny box / passion composes under the siege of general misfortune. What refreshes the heart is twofold and resorts to any gesture that might enable it to find the street where asphodels lost in their magic may stroll by. Through force or goodness a rhythmless song etches the borders of the empty circle. Aching they ache / apparitions of the skirmish between the absence and the shaft that impales its raison d'être.

XLII

Los que besan les tiran piedras a sus monstruos. La tarea de matar a la muerte cabe en una caja chica / la pasión escribe sitiada por la desdicha general. Lo que refresca al corazón es doble y acude a cualquier gesto para buscar la calle donde pasan asfódelos perdidos en su magia. Por esfuerzo o bondad una canción sin ritmo traza límites del círculo vacío. Doler duelen / apariciones del combate entre la ausencia y el dardo que la clava a su razón de ser.

XLIII

In consolation there lie false suns / the illumination is so fleeting, memory puts the wound back in its place. Loss seeks no admiration / a universe of rayless stars was devised / the slightest touch fills it with light. They give no shade, only paths / what was to what needs to be. The inharmonious groan on the corner where dispassion sanctions the world.

For Rubén Bonifaz Nuño

XLIII

En el consuelo hay soles falsos / el encandilamiento dura poco, la memoria pone a la herida en su lugar. La pérdida no busca admiración / se fabricó un universo de astros sin luz / cualquier roce lo enciende. No dan sombra, dan caminos / lo que fue a lo que falta ser. El gemido sin música en la esquina donde la despasión permite el mundo.

A Rubén Bonifaz Nuño

XLIV

Love has no face, it spends its life in ignorant stations. Darkness or filth pays it a visit now and again / pleas from the afflicted bed grow weary / the rupture of self-immersion. Behind the sky may lie another with less loss to accost each niche of the body. A night horse gallops on wounded songs and in its environs the not to be becomes surprise and enchantment. Hope is cloaked in its figures of never and the sea destroys the one that yesterday they broke off. Yesterday.

XLIV

El amor no tiene cara, vive estaciones ignorantes. La negritud o suciedad lo visita de cuando en cuando / se cansan ruegos del lecho afligido / la ruptura de la inmersión en sí. Detrás del cielo habrá otro sin tanta perdición que acecha a todas partes del cuerpo. Un caballo nocturno galopa los cantares llagados y el no ser se convierte en sorpresa y encantamiento en su morada. La esperanza se encubre en sus figuras de la nunca y el mar destruye la que ayer amputaron. Ayer.

XLV

What is this two in one? They look face to face at the world that conveys one to the other. Knives cannot penetrate the womb of a bonfire. Madness marries Eros to the dream and to death in the deciphering of things, free and mute beneath the name. They give testimony on not to be so as to be the precarious act / nakedness. What is visible cannot be imparted / the one who trembles has eyes that have glimpsed life's vacuities. The unreal that inhabits the real is the last of all stories possible.

For María Negroni

XLV

¿Qué es este dos en uno? Se miran cara a cara el mundo que carga el uno al otro. Los cuchillos no cortan la entraña de un fulgor. La locura junta a Eros con el sueño y la muerte en el desciframiento de las cosas, libres, calladas bajo el nombre. Dan testimonio del no ser para ser acto inseguro / descobijo. Lo visible es incomunicable / el que tiembla tiene ojos que vieron las ignorancias de la vida. Lo irreal que habita el real es la última de las historias posibles.

A María Negroni

XLVI

Grief opens havens / one sees what one had and faces of delight emerge. Those who are jaded by symbolic drama do not know how sorrow works shoulder to shoulder with comprehension. They study the convergence of boar and passion, woman on branch and art, assassin and death. Within the flawed desire sleep lost nights, formulas for absence, hostages of a ferocious oblivion.

For Ignacio Uranga

XLVI

El dolor abre refugios / se ve lo que se tuvo y rostros hay de la delicia. Los curtidos en dramas simbólicos ignoran cómo trabaja la pena con el entendimiento. Estudian convergencias de un jabalí con la pasión, de la mujer en rama con el arte, del asesino con la muerte. En el deseo imperfecto duermen noches perdidas, fórmulas de la ausencia, rehenes de un olvido feroz.

A Ignacio Uranga

XLVII

Present-day voids annoy the past. In the conclave of losses, some morsel of love bolsters its flame with the humble grace of what could have been. Enemies fall silent and naked nights ordain the ways / riches of the body that withstands. Storms construct alleyways, dialects, absorbing immovable codes.

XLVII

Vacíos del presente molestan al pasado. En la asamblea de las pérdidas, algún amor alza su llama con la humildad dichosa de lo que pudo ser. Los enemigos callan y la noche desnuda dicta maneras / riquezas del cuerpo que soporta. La tempestad fabrica callejones, dialectos, absorbe códigos inmóviles.

XLVIII

Loyalty to childhood tenders false information. It accompanies us, there beneath, condemned and sentenced. There are cracks in the hand that touches the street's ancient sky. Never envisioning futures, it played with stones that were ready for any and every blow. No one is heading for the terminals of what else could he have said. In the magnificent word, the soul made of flesh makes its own flesh.

XLVIII

La lealtad a la infancia es una falsa información. Nos acompaña, abajo ahí, condenada. Hay grietas en la mano que toca el cielo viejo de la calle. No esperaba futuros, jugaba con la piedra dispuesta a cualquier golpe. Nadie se va a las terminales del qué pudo decir. En la palabra espléndida, el alma hecha de carne hace su carne.

XLIX

Capitalism wants you to forget yourself, wants your very self / tú / tete-a-tete with its unbending anger / so tender. Hadewijch, softly lying there infirm, with voids you could not plumb, what shall we do with God's abyss? The breeze thickens unknown losses, and the spirit is ignorant / rods from the soul to counter one single beam of sunlight, the unpunished mistakes, beauty steals cankers from the innermost heart and trembles in the face of the victim's dread. There are no chirps / chants / toots / in the sky's trepidations. There are gunshots to come if time be willing, seas to see, the new limits of the impossible.

XLIX

El capitalismo quiere que te olvides de ti. A ti mismo / vos mismo / vos con sus broncas duras / el suave. Hadewijch, acostadita, enferma, con abismos que no pudiste penetrar, ¿qué haremos con el vacío de Dios? La brisa espesa pérdidas desconocidas y el espíritu no sabe, varas del alma contra un rayo de sol, las equivocaciones sin sufrir, la hermosura roba llagas del corazón más íntimo y tiembla en los pavores de la víctima. No hay gorjeos / cantos / silbidos / en los miedos del cielo. Hay tiros que vendrán si el tiempo deja, mares a ver, los nuevos límites de lo imposible.

L

Wrath bequeaths destitutions / they study in order to survive. No one knows how love's beds will be, the bull's melodies, the world's capability. The turtledove grieves, never to catch a glimpse. She flies from herself back to herself in pieces of the time that clothes her and she knows a great deal about the nests of here and now. Short-lived so as to leave some space.

L

La cólera lega desamparos / estudian para sobrevivir. Nadie conoce cómo serán los lechos del amor entonces, las músicas del toro, la habilidad del universo. Sufre la tórtola, nunca lo verá. Vuela de sí misma a sí misma en pedazos del tiempo que la viste y sabe mucho de nidos del momento. Dura poco para hacer lugar.

LI

The poem longs to mislead time, and grief comes round to quash it. If it were to listen to whatever flees from the door, if the imperfect light were to bear your book, betray this pain, hear your repose, if the dawn were to stumble upon the tree that once gave you shelter, if you could just come home one of these evenings.

For Marcelo

LI

El poema quiere engañar el tiempo y el sufrimiento lo derrota. Si escuchara lo que huya de la puerta, si la imperfecta luz diera tu libro, si traicionara este dolor, si oyera tu descanso, si el alba tropezara con el árbol que te abrigó una vez, si pudieras volver a casa una noche cualquiera.

A Marcelo

LII

There are lairs where love lies rotting. Freedom, freedom, cries the long-traveled road. No midnight breeze to cleanse the eye once lost, nor arm or foot fractured in the walkedness. We clip the body from the howl, advancing in outright devastation. A woman raises her arms in a sham of mercy. Beggar passion pens what fled from its pen, leaving for other desolations, other lands, and memory is a page in a bone-dry fire.

LII

Hay escondrijos donde el amor se pudre. Libertad, libertad, grita el camino caminado. Ninguna brisa a medianoche limpia el ojo perdido o brazo o pie que se rompió anduviéndolo. Recortamos el cuerpo del aullido, avanza en plena destrucción. Una mujer alza los brazos para reemplazar a la piedad. La pasión pedigüeña escribe lo que se va de su escritura a otras desolaciones, otros pagos y la memoria es un papel en fuego seco.

LIII

Oh, oh, to know with no script, taking three fingers off the madness / that spot in the landscape where patience dies. It's better you have no words and no one touch your I.T. Deportation to no port is a lovely destination / no appeals / assets / only one chasm to inhabit knowing it is deeper yet.

LIII

Hey, hey, saber sin texto, sacar tres dedos de la locura / el punto del paisaje donde mueren paciencias. Es mejor que no tengas palabras y nadie toque tu informática. El destierro sin tierra es un bello destino / sin súplicas / haberes / un solo precipicio que habitás sabiendo que es más profundo todavía.

LIV

Coordinating the soul's movements with the soul is an uncanonized act. Set your traps for happiness / following constructive projects, it will escape after stripping grips with the mechanics of infability. To feel the ground beneath your feet begets illogical splendor. Here and there the body's oeuvre is the prehistory of an origin, having sails of linen so like your mother's tablecloths / scudding sternward.

LIV

Coordinar los movimientos del alma con el alma es un acto sin ley. Tiéndanle trampas a la felicidad, saldrá con desgarrones del agarre y mecánicas de la infabilidad según proyectos constructivos. Tocar la tierra con los pies genera un esplendor sin lógica. Aquí y allá la obra del cuerpo es prehistoria de un origen, tiene velas de lino como manteles de la madre / navegan para atrás.

LV

What is the link between the concealment of death and the fluctuations of the core? Where did the wine that scrutinized lunar saliva finally wind up? The bottle lies empty on an ashen bed. Some piece of nature trades its mastery for the betrayals it won't possibly recall. A visit to the negligence that shields the being is truly worth the while. Where otherwise would the rawness of being-here sing its song? The flight left parched dew in the pulse of a child.

LV

¿Cómo se relacionan el encubrimiento de la muerte y la alternancia del adentro? ¿A dónde fue a parar el vino que investigó salivas de la luna? La botella está vacua en una cama gris. Algún pedazo de la naturaleza cambia su maestría por traiciones que no podrá reconocer. Vale la pena frecuentar los desamparos que protegen el siendo. Dónde si no cantara la crudeza de estar. Rocío seco en el pulso de un niño dejó el vuelo.

LVI

Death does not interpret his texts, does not read what he will carry off. If some prisoner at Campo de Mayo newly born mother with blindfolded eyes never to even see her child. If a robin full of wishes. If a young man reaches into the womb of a song. If he who transforms time into what-is-this. If the pain of one man in silent sobs.

LVI

La muerte no interpreta sus textos, no lee lo que se va a llevar. Si alguna prisionera en Campo de Mayo recién nacida a madre con los ojos tapados que ni a su hijo vio. Si un petirrojo que tenía deseos. Si un joven que tocaba entrañas de la música. Si el que transforma el tiempo en un qué es. Si la dolor de un hombre que llora para adentro.

LVII

Eternity has died and everything is different and you search within the impossible one. A stick immersed in water knows the mechanisms of modernity. The void toils away at its dispossession so a body can be another body, a dazzling word, labial vertigo. The eagle treads upon the snake within before granting it the flight it does not possess. The confusion of what has been created leaves time for anguish and airy hopes. The only one thinking is Love / dies young.

LVII

La eternidad ha muerto y todo es diferente y se busca en el uno imposible. El palo hundido en agua conoce la mecánica de la modernidad. El vacío trabaja en su desposesión para que un cuerpo sea otro cuerpo, una palabra que deslumbra, un vértigo labial. El águila pisa en su propia persona a la serpiente antes de darle el vuelo que no tiene. La confusión de lo creado deja tiempo al suplicio y la quimera. El único que piensa es Amor / muere joven.

LVIII

A child plays with his guts in the breathing of being-here now. The vanity of being sleeps on filthy sheets and its strategy suffers from circuits. They're constantly provoking blackouts and death calls at pale beds. The hounded dig below things, what might they find save islands locked inside an imaginary sea. Love traverses singularity equipped with small arms. It is the past, then, its charts that drive one to push on while there is still sky, the sky in its entirety, in the very corners that seek out necessary suppositions.

LVIII

Un niño juega con sus tripas en las respiraciones del estando. La pretensión de ser duerme en sábanas sucias y su estrategia sufre de circuitos. Le cortan la luz a cada rato y la muerte visita lechos pálidos. Los perseguidos cavan debajo de las cosas, qué encontrarán sino islas frenadas por un mar que no existe. El amor atraviesa la singularidad con armas cortas. Es el pasado, entonces, sus tablas que obligan a avanzar mientras hay cielo, todo el cielo, en rincones de sí que buscan suposiciones necesarias.

LIX

The cry gathers round a birth never quite born. World catastrophes penetrate the mouth and alter its decrees on tranquility. It burns, suffers, belches smoke, gives thanks for what was lost, spent. Gazing at its invisibility, it goes blind. Birds full of forest bathe a hand in the sunlight where a rusty caress lies trembling / black star / they intuit its light.

LIX

El grito se organiza alrededor del nacimiento que no termina de nacer. Catástrofes del mundo penetran en la boca y le cambian decretos de la tranquilidad. Quema, sufre, echa humo, agradece lo perdido, fue. Mira su invisibilidad y queda ciego. Pájaros llenos de bosque airean una mano donde tiembla la caricia oxidada / astro negro / adivinan su luz.

LX

Some decentered gestures never touch horizons of the flesh. Nor their shrieks, nor their hell, which reveals how handsome spectacles cower through lectures on guilt / without healthy air or the order of the parts, parts that would be love of what is not / so it may be. The harp has fallen silent in a corner full of pleas conversant with their danger. The images are singing carping furying in the deflagrations of the word and no one brings a single facet of the secret back to life. To counter reckless death, strings of spittle unfurl against a copy of the bleeding line.

LX

Hay ademanes descentrados que no tocan los horizontes de la carne. Ni sus gemidos altos, ni su infierno que enseña cómo los bellos espectáculos retroceden en las lecciones de la culpa / sin aire saludable ni el orden de las partes que amor serían de lo que no es / para que sea. Se calló el arpa en un rincón de súplicas que saben su peligro. Las imágenes cantan reniegan furian en las deflagraciones de la letra y nadie resucita un solo rasgo del secreto. Se derraman hilitos contra la muerte irresponsable en una copia de la línea borrada.

LXI

If still it were only time, love that never leaves, pain that
remains, ardent devotee, an aggregate of losses, groping
unease, dignity in conjunction with its passive organ, joy
hurled into the impassive waters of the San Fernando River.

LXI

Si todavía fuera sólo tiempo, amor que no se va, dolor
que sigue, el principal de sus discípulos, combinación de
pérdidas, desasosiegos al tanteo, la dignidad asociada a su
órgano pasivo, dicha arrojada al río San Fernando de aguas
impasibles.

LXII

Preferable to placing a glass of wine on look at the state of affairs, but where? In the theory of art regarding observers repositioned to the left? In the versions of rational choice? In the definition of rose on an empty bed? In the golden embers of accent? The magic stores are full of unsold goods, disastrous categories, the eye of a looming cyclone, the thousand other names for rain. "True life" hasn't a lick of sense to help it out / poor thing / floating up and down when the slightest breath of air passes by its you-could / if-you-were-here / you-would-have-been / you'd-be-singing on this side of the knife.

LXII

Mejor que poner un vaso de vino sobre mirá cómo son las cosas, ¿dónde? ¿En la teoría del arte sobre el observador desplazado a la izquierda? ¿En las versiones de la elección racional? ¿En la definición de rosa en un lecho vacío? ¿En ascuas de oro del acento? Los almacenes de la sorpresa están llenos de cosas sin vender, categorías desastrosas, el ojo del ciclón que va a venir, mil otros nombres de la lluvia. "La vida verdadera" no tiene un sentido que la ayude / pobre / baja y sube cuando no más que un airecito de amor pasa por sus podrías / estuvieras / fueses / cantaras de este lado del cuchillo.

LXIII

O Aristotle, Plato, Seneca, all failures at baking baguettes,
there is no sign of those all-encompassing faces, the texts
of the brotherhood, the other invention of gods. In the
conundrums of the sexual wound lie incertitudes and
fortunes, jewels of the World, the black footprints of the
self. He who fails to see his own coward is bound to enter
the vestibules of the mortaled mother. The descriptions of
loss overflow the loss, laying its weariness low. Gorgeous
that much-loved horse, his galloping legs. Kessel watched
the twilights with eyes deeper than his wound.

LXIII

Oh, Aristóteles, Platón, Séneca, fracasos en hacer pan
francés, no aparecen los rostros incluyentes, los textos de
la fraternidad, la otra invención de dioses. En los enigmas
de la herida sexual yacen incertidumbres y fortunas, joyas
del Mundo, los rastros negros de uno mismo. El que no
mira su cobarde entra en vestíbulos de la madre morida. Las
descripciones de la pérdida rebasan a la pérdida y acuestan
su cansancio. Hermoso el caballo que se amó, sus patas de
irse lejos. El Kessel miraba los crepúsculos con ojos más
hondos que su herida.

LXIV

The city melts down lost asbestos, loving as best it can. With no need to soar, it rehearses risks for souls imprisoned in the jails of reason, altering the networks of failure through failure on a long night it is loath to leave. Its thousand languages are free of obsession, possessing forests where life and death embrace free of charge. If only the love faithful to its bygone colors could bloom in this same fashion.

LXIV

La ciudad funde amiantos perdidos, ama así. No necesita volar, practica riesgos para almas presas en cárceles de la razón, cambia las relaciones del fracaso con el fracaso en una noche larga de la que no se quiere ir. Sus mil idiomas están libres de cualquier obsesión, tienen bosques frondosos en los que vida y muerte se abrazan sin pagar. Crecieran de ese modo las floraciones del amor fiel a sus colores idos.

LXV

Lasacuy, lasacuy, you mustn't let yourself flee without taking all the rest, the neighbor lady standing there in tears, whatever gobbles up little children, the alchemist's glitter devoid of golden consolation. Whatever was done in such a way was done with joyful passion, its air superb. Up and at 'em, flesh! Let us name what wants to be a name. Might death be a debt? Who knows whose groin is lugged through leaves, and the organs' purgatory is indeed acquainted with the diversity of the matter. Soul in doubt of the optic dynamism far from its sheltering chanson. Traveling to the other in order to return to the self entwines an invisible twosome. Autumn descends in honor of what was, so as not to be. There one sheds the fruitless laments, the commencements that recommence, the nights with revolvers. In innocence lie serpents.

For Jorge Boccanera

LXV

Lasacuy, lasacuy, no hay que dejarse ir a uno mismo sin el resto, la vecina que llora, lo que devora niños, los destellos del alquimista sin oros de consuelo. Lo que se hizo de tal modo fue con pasión gozosa y su aire es excelente. Arriba, carne, arriba, a nombrar lo que quiere ser nombre. ¿Será deuda la muerte? En las hojas se deslizan verijas del quién sabe y el purgatorio de los órganos conoce la variedad de la materia. Alma que duda del dinamismo óptico lejos de su mester de abrigo. Irse al otro para volver a sí enlaza dos invisibles. El otoño cae en honor de lo que fue para no ser. Ahí se pierden los lamentos inútiles, los comienzos que recomenzarán, las noches con revólver. En la inocencia hay víboras.

A Jorge Boccanera

LXVI

Amass and knead the meeting's flour, flames that burn as
they once burned, the body bereft of history in the dark of
night. You must enter the dissonant cages, muster diverse
tenses, observe the dearth or parity of languages that do not
sound the same with the same. A word goes here and there,
seeking a place one would never leave. Impossible, its only
house / one that none will build.

LXVI

Amásense harinas del encuentro, llamas que arden como
ardieron, el cuerpo sin historia cada noche. Penétrense
las jaulas inarmónicas, júntese tanta variedad de tiempos,
mírese lo que falta o paridad de idiomas que no suenan lo
mismo con lo mismo. La palabra va de aquí para allá, busca
un sitio de no marcharse nunca. Su única casa es imposible,
nadie se la va a construir.

LXVII

The tongue's fables visit gelid lairs. Forever dark they hold surprises / fear / ignorance / envy / a fetid devil's tail. What could be better than *mainumbí* for the butterflies to float in the spirit's hemispheres? In Huauquipura the brothers do Quechua, and the quinces in the grove quash death with their scent. In the mechanics of time there are words that refuse to expose themselves, unpunished gods, ancient ruins of new-found love. Parting digs holes leaving no valediction.

For Teresa Franco

LXVII

Las fábulas de la lengua visitan rincones sin calor. Siempre es oscuro allí y sorpresa / temor / ignorancia / recelo / la cola de un demonio rancio. ¿Qué mejor que *mainumbí* para que mariposas vuelen en hemisferios del espíritu? En huakepura hacen quechua los hermanos y el membrillo del monte derrota muertes con su aroma. En las mecánicas del tiempo hay palabras que no se dejan ver, dioses impunes, ruinas viejas del nuevo amor. La partida cava pozos sin discurso.

A Teresa Franco

LXVIII

How does one enter the darkness of conscience, its intentional stones, the borders of its mirrors. Beauty lies mute beside the man infected with the times. Who, in the presence of stupidity's spawn, gouged out her eyes? Her rancor swiftly recedes into the organs of reason. The future is saddened with unthinkable thoughts and the goldfinch sings in flights bound to vanish. The violent fantasies within are upwardly cruel, their utility is treason and no one tills the lands of dread. Wind sweeps the desert sand, glimmers of evil, say what you will regarding love's independence.

For José Ángel Leyva

LXVIII

Cómo entrar en la oscuridad de la conciencia, sus piedras a propósito, la delimitación de sus espejos. La belleza se calla junto al enfermo de la época. ¿Quién le clavó cegueras ante las criaturas de la estupidez? Sus rencores caen rápido en órganos de la razón. El futuro está triste en pensamientos impensables y los jilgueros cantan en vuelos que se irán. Las fantasías violentas del adentro son crueles hacia arriba, su utilidad es traición y nadie labra las tierras del espanto. El viento barre la arena del desierto, los fulgores del mal, dígase lo que se diga de autonomías del amor.

A José Ángel Leyva

LXIX

Oblivion founders in the swells of desire / the dawn that trembled during a firefight / the crescent moon cut away from a night re-lifed in its protraction. What fills the indictments of horror? Beasts that offer up their vigor roam fields long-gone, and another tatter can be heard falling from the world. The debt of what we never were will never be repaid, it dallies about with its mirroring fears signed and sealed. The space is filled with the disobedience of a sparrow.

LXIX

El olvido encalla en movimientos del deseo / la madrugada que tembló en un combate / la media luna cortada de la noche vol-vida a su prolongación. ¿Qué llena los sumarios del espanto? Bestias que ofrecen su energía recorren campos idos y se oye cómo cae otro harapo del mundo. La deuda con lo que no fuimos nunca se pagará, anda por áhi con su espejo de miedos sellados. El espacio se llena con la desobediencia de un gorrión.

LXX

The instant of the body's act dedicates its congress to the world. Lovers sit at the foot of the poplars not being, fabricating horizons for a muddled Eden and leaving their ways of doing alongside autumn. Injustice has already arrived in her cross-filled carriage, her homeless unspirit. O how Coucy's nightingales sing *in thoughts barred by beauty*. The soulbody refuses to surrender and its pendulum swings from falsehood to truth like some forsaken rage.

LXX

El instante del acto corporal dedica al mundo su congreso. Los amantes se sientan al pie de álamos no siendo, fabrican horizontes para un Edén confuso y dejan su manera de hacer al lado del otoño. Ya vino la injusticia en su carro de cruces, su desespíritu sin techo. Cómo cantan los ruiseñores de Coucy *en pensamientos que la hermosura cesa*. El cuerpoalma no capitula y su péndulo pasa de la mentira a la verdad como una furia sola.

LXXI

Chance severs the guts of corruption, Power passes by and
sutures the gash. Beneath still lie beating the impotence of
the poor, alphabets for the ineffable now fled, treaties of a
reason broken and tamed. Lying alongside the human rights
of the past, those of the present bleed unsheltered. Cruelty
claws with capable nails. The country's chasms paint them
red and its institutions give a standing ovation. The garden
watered by Love shudders with fear. What's the worth of
a life not lost in future salts. It preserves its ruins and so
survives.

LXXI

El azar corta las entrañas de la corrupción, pasa el Poder y
cierra la heridaza. Laten adentro impotencias del pobre, las
letras de lo inefable huido, tratados de la razón domada. Al
lado de los derechos humanos del pasado sangran sin abrigo
los derechos humanos del presente. La crueldad usa uñas
buenas. Los agujeros del país las pintan con esmalte rojo
y las instituciones felicitan de pie. Tiembla el jardín que
Amor regaba. De qué vale la vida que no se perdió en sales
del futuro. Cuida sus ruinas y sobrevive así.

LXXII

The heart's elastic leap to its never having been performs time's oeuvres with utter resolve. Who do they think they are those hours gone by? Do they not drag the ebb and flow of a death bereft of bones? Seas one may as well keep, bring what they may. In the longstanding sadness there is the love that is there, lost flames embrace its affliction. Learn to keep your hands off programmed wisdom, faithless beasts. The vertical axis does not separate the war from the horse, desire from the thing desired, the tender heart from its hardness. We are orphans of letters we can no longer send.

LXXII

El salto elástico del corazón a su no sido ejecuta con intención obras del tiempo. ¿Qué se creen las horas que pasaron? ¿No arrastran flujos y reflujos de una muerte sin huesos? Mares que mejor quedárselos, traigan lo que traigan. En la vieja tristeza hay el amor que hay, fuegos perdidos abrazan su aflicción. Quiten las manos del saber automático, animales sin fe. El eje vertical no separa a la guerra del caballo, al deseo de la cosa deseada, al blando corazón de su dureza. Estamos huérfanos de cartas que no se pueden enviar.

LXXIII

When God gathered together all the letters to begin the world, one of them was truant. Wandering waif / she seeks out a mouth as a haven. Not even fasting helps to behold her, ever traveling in her thirst for justice. In the eye she hewed her absence, no decree to found her and no one finds her sound. She shines within, a vertigo unseen where I am cantering in you. Even voids remain invisible, no matter how many edicts are issued. Thought-packs are assembled to ensure more blood on the streets while a single sky in the prehistory of this night sings on. We hunger for the secret of a pain made of wood we consign to the fire.

LXXIII

Cuando Dios juntó a las letras para empezar el mundo, faltó una a la reunión. Vaga / busca boca que la abrigue. Ni ayunos sirven para haberla, viaja y viaja esperando justicia. En el ojo cavó su ausencia, ningún decreto la establece y nadie encuentra su sonido. Brilla adentro y no le ven el vértigo donde yo en vos cabalgo. La nada propia es invisible por más anuncios que le pongan. Se fabrican paquetes de pensar para que haya más sangre por las calles y todavía canta un firmamento en la prehistoria de esta noche. Tenemos hambre del secreto donde el dolor es de madera y se echa al fuego.

LXXIV

The joys of the *cerulean void that wets your clothes* have traveled across centuries of human voices. Here they are, in hand an artless rose that knows how not to know. In the ignorance of itself it allows future luminosity to flourish. Thus, it gains possession of the instant of dispossession, inside the outer passion returned to its passion. What wants to be a name patrols the hoarfrost of being here. It enjoys the awe of a student who doesn't learn the convenience of handy cold-heartedness, the gloom of gold or abandoned flesh, the book of fears. In the rapture of the cerulean void all is promise / the hurdles of deceit / the lunar tenderness floating in misfortune / the black beingness that persists.

For François Cheng

LXXIV

Las alegrías del *vacío azul que moja la ropa* atravesaron siglos de la voz humana. Aquí están, con una rosa natural en la mano que sabe no saber. En la ignorancia de sí misma deja crecer fulgores que vendrán. Así posee el instante de la desposesión, adentro la pasión de afuera devuelta a su pasión. Lo que quiere ser nombre patrulla fríos del estar. Tiene asombros de alumno que no aprende los desamores que convienen, las tinieblas del oro o carne abandonada, el libro de los miedos. En las delicias del azul vacío todo es promesa / los imposibles del engaño / la suavidad lunar que vuela en la desdicha / el siendo oscuro que persiste.

A François Cheng

LXXV

In the madness of return there's a room containing rivers. Taking their turns at the helm there are sobs, an absolute of plain percale, dialogues of yesses and noes in various niches of the shade. Blood nears its forks and mulls the services error provides. Chance doesn't ever want to leave. Undefeated mortal beauty hangs lessons on the line like laundry out to dry and its miracle falls mute, dangling fiery hours the size of what you once had been. The responses of a limping harmony collide with firing squads. The dream, two alone in a nook to write. The sea / the sea.

LXXV

Hay una habitación que tiene ríos en las locuras del regreso. La navegan sollozos, un absoluto de percal, diálogos del sí y el no en las diversas partes de la sombra. La sangre se acerca a sus derivaciones y contempla servicios del error. El azar nunca se quiere ir. Hermosura mortal no vencida tiende lecciones como ropa y su milagro calla, cuelga horas ardientes del tamaño que fuiste. Los intercambios de la armonía renga chocan con las fusilaciones. El sueño es dos solos en un rincón de la escritura. El mar / el mar.

LXXVI

May they frighten off what's lost, may the mercury silence what it knows, vivat, vivat, may the soups bring me the mother of moist movements. Of all the colors of the spectrum the one that twists the struggle's ire has gone missing. Gray world in gray speculations and the poor gaze at stars that never step into their homes. Glimmers of Ruth say leave yourself to go to yourself, and misery's music shines in shapeless songs. The gunpowder the enemies sense reeks of unforgivable jasmine.

For Eduardo Galeano

LXXVI

Que repeluznen lo perdido, que el mercurio no diga lo que sabe, vivat, vivat, que las sopas me traigan a la madre de movimientos húmedos. En los colores del espectro falta el que tuerce iras de la lucha. El mundo gris en especulaciones grises y el pobre mira astros que no entran en su casa. Los destellos de Ruth dicen vete de vos a vos mismo y músicas de la miseria brillan en cantos sin contorno. La pólvora que huele el enemigo tiene jazmines sin perdón.

A Eduardo Galeano

LXXVII

Pollen pushes open hospital doors and hovers over dirty
sheets. That one, the other one there. What might they
want to eat of him that he himself, injected with ending,
hasn't already eaten. There's no alternate key to blue heaven
/ blood interred for being-here and being-here now again.
The ship is sailing laden with pieces of the error in its brutal
silence untouched.

LXXVII

El polen abre la puerta de los hospitales y sobrevuela sábanas
sucias. Aquél, aquél. Que le querrán comer que él mismo
no se comió con inyecciones del final. No hay llave alterna
al cielo azul / sangre tapada por el estar y estar. Se va la nave
cargada de piezas del error en su bruto silencio intocado.

LXXVIII

Power's erections enjoy no ecstasy, its voracity garners no verbal gold. Sailing in the clocks of its dissolution are sunken-prowed ships, rusted images of pinioned plumes, bastardly parliaments. In observing the sun multiple eyes are born, distant countries hemorrhage as proof and the act of insisting eats up the very bread it bakes. Freedom denied doesn't expire so young, it explores the fringes of possibility. Chance reveals strange organs with inextinguishable light.In the end, so much wretchedness, so much flight traceless yet.

For Eric Nepomuceno

LXXVIII

Las erecciones del Poder no tienen éxtasis, su codicia no junta oros del lenguaje. En los relojes de su disolución navegan barcos de proa hundida, imágenes oxidadas de plumas bien cortadas, parlamentos canallas. La observación del sol crea ojos múltiples, se derraman países lejanos en su virtud de prueba y el acto de insistir come del pan que horneó. La libertad negada no se muere tan joven, explora las posibilidades del confín. El azar muestra órganos extraños con luz inapagable. Tanta miseria finalmente, tanto vuelo sin huella todavía.

A Eric Nepomuceno

LXXIX

The fruit of the jungle, of the Pampas, of the seas spiraling down into inglorious hungers. Eternity's accusations wager their wrinkles, a lawless weariness remains. How is a man to be conjoined with the one they have made of him? He sees his ambiguities / they leave his eyes half shut. Loss broils organs in broad daylight, in the broad mouth of personations. Old love is fulfilled in the termination that recreates it.

LXXIX

Lo mejor de las selvas, las pampas y los mares cae en hambres sin gloria. Las delaciones de la eternidad arriesgan sus arrugas, un cansancio que se quedó sin leyes. ¿Cómo se junta un hombre con el que le hicieron? Se mira ambigüedades / entrecierran los ojos. La pérdida cuece órganos en pleno día, en plena boca de las personaciones. El viejo amor se cumple en la terminación que lo recrea.

LXXX

Utopia's guts have no coordinates. Advancing along the eastern border of the beasts and in the sierras of Córdoba / it is watered by many a vein / losing battles / living with hunger. Thoughts are more cloaked in fogs than is the body and their variables never pluck the lyre. Where did the whole go? Toward its fragments, its overflowing void / does it reckon with broken buskers? In the processions from **a** to **z**, you find them elbowing one another, that old beggar woman, flesh sacrificed for distribution, the evenhanded on the street. Reason has gone rancid.

For Rogelio Blanco

LXXX

El estómago de la utopía no tiene coordenadas. Avanza por el lado oriental de las bestias y en un monte de Córdoba / regado por muchas sangres / pierde batallas / pasa hambre. El pensamiento tiene más nieblas que el cuerpo y sus variables nunca tocan la lira. ¿A dónde se fue el todo? ¿A sus pedazos, a su vacío lleno, saca cuentas con saltimbanquis rotos? En procesiones de la a **a** la **z** se codean la mendiga, carne sacrificada a repartir, los justos en la calle. La razón se echó a perder.

A Rogelio Blanco

LXXXI

Folks clad in horrendous hypotheses ignore the fact that horses mature and their corners are stomping, nibbling pap at grandma's side, and in their gravitational fields the invisible is blooming. They decipher pulmonary vibes. You can hear them in preceding tasks, demolishing absolutes and covenants with scientific circles, lounging in what they are going to be. A breath brought them into the world with pages composed by the sun. All around the male, time is tuning its silences, the female sings them, the toddler finds his footing to shun repetitions.

For Jean Portante

LXXXI

Los revestidos de hipótesis terribles ignoran que los caballos crecen y sus rincones piafan, comen papa al costado de la abuela y en su campo gravitacional florece lo invisible. Descifran vibraciones del pulmón. Se los oye en trabajos precedentes, destruyen absolutos y pactos con círculos científicos, se acuestan en lo que van a ser. Un aliento los vino al mundo con páginas que el sol escribe. Alrededor del macho el tiempo afina sus silencios, la hembra los canta, el niño se pone en pie para evitar repeticiones.

A Jean Portante

LXXXII

Language is a bone drifting at leisure before possessing the son. While pausing it feasts on the infinite and its bond with universal desire embraces the discontinuity it names. Free in suspensions of the origin, it kens its duration the moment it departs. The innocence of the circle hangs heavy upon it, so much misery all around. It penetrates incomplete unities. So many words disowned, longing for a cradle.

For Jacques Ancet

LXXXII

El lenguaje es un hueso, vaga a su antojo antes de poseer al hijo. En sus pausas se come al infinito y su enlace con el deseo mundial abarca la discontinuidad que nombra. Es libre en suspensiones del origen, conoce su duración en el instante que se fue. Le pesa la inocencia del círculo, tanta miseria alrededor. Penetra las unidades incompletas. Cuánta palabra echada atrás esperando una cuna.

A Jacques Ancet

LXXXIII

There are neither coins nor change in God's tomb, only the chasm's cradle, lay ignorance aside all ye who enter. Desire is freed of tattoos under the moon that bathed in the river / such absence / barbarity / beasts feasting on the heart. Not one bird's flight can be heard for now, nor are there shadows or anything else to fill that infinity. From *finis mare* havenless ships set sail, qualms that left their homes, the ambivalence of the quake. The quality of variability goes blind in the face of humanity's traceless blue. The letter below will not sate the sadness. The timeworn page is waiting for truth to write what it does not know.

For Herbert Frey

LXXXIII

No hay monedas ni cambio en la tumba de Dios, está la cuna del vació, dejad toda ignorancia ustedes que entran. El deseo se libra de tatuajes bajo la luna que se mojó en el río y tanta ausencia / tanta barbaridad / tanta bestia comiendo el corazón. Ningún vuelo de pájaro se escucha todavía, ni sombras hay ni nada que ocupe esa infinidad. Del *finis mare* parten naves sin puerto, los temores que dejaron su casa, ambivalencias del temblor. La cualidad de lo variable está ciega ante el azul sin huellas de lo humano. La carta abajo no es suficiente por tristeza. El papel viejo espera que la verdad escriba todo lo que no sabe.

A Herbert Frey

LXXXIV

Amid the fragments of the symbolic process there is dry
blood from Dock Sud. Where else would that sheen come
from, the four terms of metaphor, the oxymoron the
scholars explore? The *compañeros* of furthermore composed
themselves with gunshots in a sundown of impossible
transformation. In their silence a law that kills poverty falls
mute. And oh how they brandished fantasies to banish evil
to another universe, to empty streets where they fell in love.
Death came to bear them out.

For Nicole Gdalia

LXXXIV

En los fragmentos del proceso simbólico hay sangre seca
del Dock Sur. ¿De ánde si no les vienen brillo, los cuatro
términos de la metáfora, el oxímoron que estudian
profesores? Los compañeros del también se calmaron a tiros
en un ocaso sin transformación posible. En su silencio calla
una ley que mata a la pobreza. Y cómo alzaban fantasías
para que se moviera la maldad a otro universo, desocupara
calles donde amaron. La muerte vino a darles la razón.

A Nicole Gdalia

LXXXV

Thinking gives shape to a flower that amuses death. Hand in hand they sit at the foot of the harshest of autumn trees and nowhere else can this volume of valor be found. Upon the linen tablecloth a bowl of soup falls mute, and no one opens the open door. Outside dogs bark beyond their dog and decisive discourse comes to an end. The moon travels on waters that move from the heart to midnights of the winched, immobile in another winding down.

LXXXV

El pensamiento hace una flor que entretiene a la muerte. Las dos se juntan al pie del árbol más severo del otoño y en ningún otro lugar cabe tanto valor. En el mantel de lino calla un plato de sopa y nadie abre la puerta abierta. Afuera ladran perros más allá de su perro y se acaba el discurso decisivo. La luna viaja en aguas que van del corazón a medianoches del sacado, muy quieto en otro acábase.

LXXXVI

The self shores up its others with groaning rebar. The turtledove's penultimate center detaches itself from the turtledove, countries of the end where structures tumble down / outlandish nights worm their way in / whims of the landscape. The foot falls awakening the witness's obsessions / an eccentric spirit hunts itself down to discover who it is.

LXXXVI

El yo repara sus otros con fierros que sollozan. El penúltimo centro de una tórtola se aleja de la tórtola, países del final donde las estructuras se derriban / entran noches ajenas / antojos del paisaje. El paso despierta las obsesiones del testigo / un espíritu extraño se persigue para saber quién es.

LXXXVII

The pulse crosses the being-here like a moonless Tyche. A rainfall recites its thousand nameless faces and maddens the tongue that seeks them out. Tatters fall from the being, disillusions with nowhere to hide, ah sweet and fleeting May. Where does the drift-perturbing fog call home? They have crushed the return of ferns where, sunless, nothing could occur.

For André Velter

LXXXVII

El pulso cruza el estar como tyké sin luna. Una lluvia recita sus mil rostros sin nombre y enloquece la lengua que los busca. Caen del ser harapos, desilusiones sin rincón, ay dulce mayo que te vas. ¿Dónde vive la niebla que desordena la deriva? Han rompido la vuelta a los helechos donde nada sin sol podía suceder.

A André Velter

LXXXVIII

The moon is born in the pallor of fields of flax, returning in colors that travel with their own calm. Eros glistened against skies denied / in clandestine cables. There are children who ask if words erase the things that hurt / erect ruins with boulder intention / end not how they ended. The soil polishes bones that time steals never to give back.

For Lucila Pagliai

LXXXVIII

La luna nace en la blancura del linar. Vuelve en colores que viajan con calmas de sí mismos. Eros brilló contra cielos negados y en cables clandestinos. Hay niños que preguntan si la palabra tacha lo que sufre / levanta ruinas con intención de roca / no se acaba en lo que se acabó. La tierra pule huesos que el tiempo roba sin retorno.

A Lucila Pagliai

LXXXIX

During my childhood one of the city's trees burst into
song. Its young shoots entertained thoughts I cannot think.
Born between the table and the gaze are times of cold, of
goodness, of fear, tracks, marks, with room for horror now
and again. Someone is rinsing the tears that grew in his
hands. Afternoon enlists market remains, unnamed circles,
husks of ancient combat, the hazy zither of the plan to
ensure that night might be and its beast be splendid.

For Joaquín Sabina

LXXXIX

Un árbol de la ciudad cantó en mi infancia. Sus brotes
jóvenes pensaron lo que no sé pensar. Entre la mesa y la
mirada nace el tiempo del frío, de la bondad, del miedo,
huellas, marcas, cupo el espanto alguna vez. Alguien enjuga
lágrimas que le crecieron en la mano. La tarde recluta restos
del mercado, círculos sin denominación, exteriores de los
viejos combates, la vihuela borrosa del propósito para que
noche sea y su animal espléndido.

A Joaquín Sabina

XC

So many faces in the void left by God. Those that lash the sunset to their appellations misconstrue the backsides of their shadows. Personal self-sufficiencies till the lands of bewilderment, repetitions that will appear in moments conversant with their wounds. There are laundresses for the future at long-suffering lakes and revelations for the present. A lovely peril glimmers in every prison, freedom at the door with wings that must be crafted.

XC

Cuántos rostros en el vacío que Dios dejó. El que amarra el ocaso a su designación equivoca el revés de su sombra. Autonomías personales aran los territorios de la equivocación, repeticiones que vendrán con instantes que entiendan sus heridas. Hay lavanderas del futuro en lagos resignados y confidencias del presente. Un hermoso peligro brilla en cada prisión, la libertad en la puerta con alas que hay que hacer.

XCI

Scientific projects, academic precariousness, cross-purposed vindications, norms of visibility, Papal paranoia, do not delune the moon. Her animal scent remains regardless of mathematics / comforting illusions reach a dead end in all our global fury. The link between lightning and human pain illumines the wounds in one blue flash. Rifles should be blooming in the peat of being upon wishing to be. They have left the scene / the assassin, still scot-free.

For Philippe Ollé

XCI

El empleo científico, la precariedad académica, las reivindicaciones transversales, las normas de la visibilidad, la paranoia de los Papas, no deslunan la luna. Ella tiene perfumes de animal sin matemáticas y las ilusiones confortables van al muere en la furia del mundo. Las relaciones del relámpago con el dolor humano iluminan heridas en un instante azul. Debieran florecer fusiles en los musgos del ser al querer ser. Se fueron de la escena / el asesino quedó libre.

A Philippe Ollé

XCII

Living in things deposes the pen. They will not write on those nights when time is fixed. The names they possess navigate the tongue, sounds long sought. Free in a silent seat, on a tabling table, they cannot change the syntagmas of their mute lunacy. He who seeks out his pasts finds himself stranded on parallel rocks. They live in bulls / the tablecloth / the soup / the canter of horses acquainted with their wine, and no one takes a sip.

XCII

Vivir adentro de las cosas destituye su pluma. No escribirían en las noches donde fijan el tiempo. Tienen nombres que navegan la lengua, sonidos que se buscan. Libres en una silla callada, una mesa que mesa, no cambian los sintagmas de su locura muda. Quien busca sus pasados encalla en rocas paralelas. Viven en toros / el mantel / la sopa / galopes de caballos que conocen su vino y nadie bebe.

XCIII

Nostalgia drops anchor in consummated hemistiches and
something is born in its unwinding. What has occurred has
something not yet occurred and no one reads its tidings.
Structures lie / they want to strangle what's still alive / to use
politics to kill splendors. The missing shots will come / the
sky will net the virtue covering us all / speculum for the gift
/ the day that never came.

XCIII

La nostalgia ancla en hemistiquios sucedidos y algo nace de
su desplegación. Lo que pasó tiene algo que todavía no pasó
y nadie lee sus noticias. Las estructuras mienten / quisieran
apagar lo que está vivo / usan políticas para matar bellezas.
Vendrán los tiros que faltaron / el cielo redará la virtud que
a todos cubre / espéculos del don / el día que no vino más.

XCIV

Without knowing till when I had bid you farewell. I
returned with holes that hushed exilic rhythms, music that
forbids its recreation, a tree of falling leaves that frighten off
the birds. They return to the clouds still left me. Shots in
the chest are forever young, free of shame, mists that rained.

XCIV

Sin saber hasta cuándo me despedí de vos. Volví con
agujeros donde callaban compases del exilio, una música
que no se deja recrear, un árbol del que caen hojas que
asustan a los pájaros. Vuelven a nubes que me quedan. Tiros
del pecho siguen jóvenes, libres de su vergüenza, neblinas
que llovieron.

XCV

A residue of evil remains on the hand that shot the enemy. With what goodness is injustice killed? The bloom-eating bird leaves a stain on time's deeds / the sea rejects love gone bad. The monetary spirit is the flesh of violent slavery. It rapes the land that was its king as a child. It will die without honor when Beowulf returns to brandish his sword against the venomous flames / miscarried springs / not a soul in the hall of names.

XCV

En la mano que disparó al enemigo hay restos de maldad. ¿Con qué bondad se mata a la injusticia? El pájaro que come flores mancha actos del tiempo / el mar no acepta amor que mal termina. El espíritu económico es carne de esclavitud violenta. Viola el paisaje que le fue rey de niño. Morirá sin honor cuando Beowulf vuelva a blandir su espada contra los fuegos venenosos / las primaveras malparidas / nadie en la sala de los nombres.

XCVI

Every toddler suffers the wound they've inflicted and learns
the art of hearing, ear to the loam of the tongue, listening
to the fluctuations of amorous pacts. Relegating savage
traditions, he enters his unknowing without reasoned
successions and never dodges the death that happened by.
He plots omens that will tell him who he is, free of images
that might shroud his efforts, moving on to his latest hell
where a mockingbird warbles how to muddle through.

XCVI

El niñito que nace sufre la herida que le hicieron, aprende el
arte de oír sobre los suelos de la lengua y escucha el vaivén
de los pactos de amor. Aparta tradiciones salvajes, entra en
su desconocimiento sin sucesiones razonadas y no esquiva
a la muerte que pasó. Traza signos que le dirán quién es sin
imágenes que cubran su fuerza del trabajo. Pasa a su nuevo
infierno donde una calandria canta cómo irse mejor.

XCVII

Misery's rage forges the bullets to come. This / for a doe's
upright love of song. Donning scarlet sandals, heavenly
bodies stroll upon the fields of flax where the sun lies down
to rest / the poor man's sole possession needs so few words.
Love begs inside out / suffering from the world's mistakes
/ gunshots curdle, thicken. The tongue listens in mute
desperation.

XCVII

El furor de la miseria funde las balas que vendrán. Esto
ocurrió por justo amor a la música de un ciervo. Astros
caminan con sandalias rojas sobre el linar donde se acuesta
el sol / lo único del pobre usa pocas palabras. Amor pide en
su reverso / padece los errores del mundo / hay tiros que se
espesan. Los escucha la lengua con desesperos mudos.

XCVIII

The future died young in the blood's adventures. It possessed fresh pages with neither protection nor peace. In the imitations of its loss, love is a lost dog. The old clock is sad and dead leaves begin to fall. Behind its ticking there are trees that have never slept / that understood the night / the error's hatchet strokes. The marrow of the fallen feeds the rumors of a rose.

XCVIII

El futuro se murió joven en aventuras de la sangre. Tuvo páginas nuevas sin protección ni calma. En las imitaciones de su pérdida el amor es un perro perdido. El viejo reloj está triste y caen hojas muertas. Detrás de su sonido hay árboles que no durmieron / entendieron la noche / hachazos del error. Las médulas de los caídos dan de comer a los rumores de una rosa.

XCIX

Ruins from the refuge foster sightless souls. What does memory rearrange in its desire? Fate disarranges symbols, and in one single bloom the loneliest of passion's remains drops anchor, midnight looking on. The landscape migrates to its invisible land, calm in the labors of the tongue. The shriek has died down and selects its recollections, forehead that broke walls to peer over, the struggle's quiet mornings, fear's evaporations. Hand over hand the future holds fast to the humble miracle of a hope the calendars refuse to visit. Iron threads stitch what is ending to what has ended and stamp the garments with other labels.

XCIX

Las ruinas del refugio cultivan seres ciegos. ¿Qué reordena la memoria en su deseo? El azar desorganiza símbolos y en una flor anclan restos de la pasión más sola, la medianoche que los ve. Migra el paisaje a su invisible, quieto en trabajos de la lengua. El gemido murió y elige los recuerdos, la frente que rompía muros para mirar arriba, mañanas sigilosas de la lucha, las evaporaciones del temor. El futuro retiene soga a soga al humilde milagro de la espera que no visitan calendarios. Hilos de fierro cosen lo que se acaba con lo que se acabó y en la ropa escriben otra cosa.

C

Memory has mishaps all the time / sweeping away continuums, passing from its active center to the disarticulations of the masks. It bleeds as the world bleeds and its certainties collapse into quicklime. In the oblivion of forgetting there is no rest, he who died dies yet again and livid blows repel the conjugations of escape. Cold saliva in the bonfire where those who ripped out the blank page now stand burning. In the goodness of deceit cyclones molder. Love twirls and twirls in the blindest of circles, the only thing left.

C

La memoria sufre accidentes cada vez / barre continuos y pasa de su centro activo a desarticulaciones de las máscaras. Sangra como sangra el mundo y sus certezas caen en cal viva. En el olvido de olvidar no hay descanso, el que murió muere otra vez y golpes lívidos cocean a las conjugaciones de la fuga. Saliva fría de la hoguera donde arden los que arrancaron la hoja blanca. En las bondades del engaño se pudren los ciclones. El amor gira y gira en el círculo más ciego, lo único que queda.

CI

And if the southern winds had a metal forest? And if the red clay in Misiones fired disasters? And if the Talmud had stroked my grandfather's beard? And if on muddy fields a pure rose should grow and the spirit be a dot with no be? And if the structures, the coordination, the communication were the daytime remains of the void? And if misery be the future's oblivion? And if on the memorials of entrance there be concentric faces in age-old modesty? And if in the collapse of understanding, virgin passions were to flourish? And if the knot of lies were to come loose in natural rivers and eternity's failure begin to speak out? In time's erogenous zones?

CI

¿Y si el viento del sur tuviera un bosque de metal? ¿Y si la tierra roja de Misiones calcinara desastres? ¿Y si el Talmud roza las barbas del abuelo? ¿Y si en campos de fango crece una rosa pura y el espíritu es un punto sin es? ¿Y si las estructuras, las coordinaciones, las comunicaciones fueran los restos diurnos del vacío? ¿Y si las miserias sean olvidos del futuro? ¿Y si en los memoriales de la entrada habrá rostros concéntricos en un pudor antiguo? ¿Y si en clausuras del entendimiento crecen pasiones vírgenes? ¿Y si el nudo de la mentira se deshiciera en ríos naturales y hable el fracaso de la eternidad? ¿En las zonas erógenas del tiempo?

CII

Language takes a seat next to night and reviews its creatures.
When that order collapses, the hole swallows its whole.
Leaving debts unpaid, it will speak of the fate that each
thing invents. No one lends it dawns and its ruins suck all
the air out of the air. The methodologies of the past change
with one flower that blooms and lasts with those who
witness it unseen. Neither bird nor song nor summer leaf
can detach one's mind from cleaning the pasterns of the
horse that gallops best.

CII

El lenguaje se sienta al lado de la noche y repasa sus
criaturas. Cuando ese orden se derrumba, el aujero bebe su
aujero. No pagará sus deudas, hablará del azar que toda cosa
inventa. Nadie le presta amaneceres y sus ruinas le quitan
aire al aire. Las metodologías del pasado cambian con una
flor que crece, dura mucho y hay testigos de que no se ve.
Ni pájaro ni silbo ni hoja del verano separa a la cabeza de
limpiar las ranillas del caballo que galopa mejor.

CIII

The trek from possibility to impossibility is full of nightbound ohs / vestiges of nightingales, their songs of old, gods who lied, hemorrhages of evidence, the rusted generosity of musty thoughts. When will they lift the lid on being's self-ignorance, weeds growing slowly so as not to make a sound? Bring your sharpened machetes / long-tusked boars. The eclipse of duality is brief, and it is not from sorrow that the sigh remains, uncowering in the face of a ravaging center. In the mother's steppes there were admonitions of amorphous tragedy. Mazes of time behind the times remain. They chopped off the hands of the panacean forget-me-not, which blooms yet today.

For Antonio Gamoneda

CIII

El tránsito de la posibilidad a la imposibilidad está lleno de ayes de la noche. Hay restos de ruiseñores que cantaron temprano ahí, hay dioses que mintieron, derrames de la demostración, la generosidad oxidada de viejos pensamientos. ¿Cuándo levantarán la tapa del no saberse del ser, las malezas que le crecen despacio para no hacer ruido? Traigan machetes de buen filo / jabalíes. Los eclipses de la dualidad duran poco y no es de pena su suspiro insumiso a un centro que lo coma. En las llanuras de la madre había advertencias de la tragedia amorfa. Quedan laberintos de tiempo detrás del tiempo. Le cortaron la mano al elixir del nomeolvides que crece todavía.

A Antonio Gamoneda

CIV

In the recurrence of error fear prevails. Was each fury a lightning bolt conjoining worlds? Was every danger there present in the watering of fronds where newborn finches were to sing? Divided days lose their count. The multiplication of questions trims lunar plumes / some sparrows prefer the fire / whitened winds / genuine shame. Poetry doesn't know how to hover leisurely over the chasm and no one can cleave it from what it is but isn't. Lying below, natural sciences, anxiety, death's numbers, the horrendous drought that ensued.

CIV

En los regresos del error hay miedo todavía. ¿Cada furia era un rayo que juntaba mundos? ¿Cada peligro era regar la fronda donde iban a cantar jilgueros próximos? Los días divididos no saben contar. La multiplicación de las preguntas corta plumas lunares / hay gorriones que prefieren el fuego / vientos blancos / vergüenzas de verdad. La poesía no sabe holgar sobre el abismo y nadie puede separarla de lo que es pero no es. Abajo hay ciencias naturales, ansias, números de la muerte, la seca atroz que vino.

CV

What is the origin in this world of awkward persuasions.
Did it flee in the dialects of dawn's early light? Cross the
Andes on horseback? Does it have a mirror to look at
doubts? Write letters never to be sent? Perform its spectacle
with no clue? In the heavenly choirs it shows not a hint
of resignation, mute as a forlorn philosophy. The eagle
recognizes such forbearance when his mate takes to washing
the dirty laundry.

CV

Qué es el origen en este mundo de persuasiones torpes.
¿Huyó en dialectos de la aurora? ¿Cruzó los Andes a caballo?
¿Tiene un espejo donde mira dudas? ¿Escribe cartas que
no envía? ¿Despliega su espectáculo sin llave? En los coros
celestes no hay señales de su resignación, calla como triste
teoría. La reconoce el águila cuando la águila lava la ropa
sucia.

CVI

Faces not departing from where they were going / populate the dispersion of the invisible. Relative reality brings rains that sound different on roofs of zinc and those of solitude. No one gives them a name. Intermediary organs distill the object's blindness / currency of the appeal. The logical relations of the movement lie like little children. Scientific fifes resound intoning the desolation and misery that time will fill with wrinkles.

CVI

Rostros que no se van de lo que iban / pueblan la dispersión de lo invisible. La relativa realidad trae lluvias que no suenan lo mismo contra un techo de zinc y otro de soledad. Nadie les pone nombre. Órganos intermediarios destilan cegueras del objeto / divisas del recurso. Las relaciones lógicas del movimiento mienten como niñitos. Suenan los pífanos científicos sobre desolaciones y miserias que el tiempo arruga.

CVII

Desire born of deserts is garbed in rags / drinks its wailings / misfortunes tug. They give it a cradle and it sleeps in the decree. It's acquainted with the cruelty of sweetness and grows without a trace of infinity.

CVII

Deseo que nace de un desierto viste harapos / bebe sus lloros / desgracias tiran para atrás. Son su cuna y duerme en la enunciación. Conoce la crueldad de la dulzura y crece sin infinito alguno.

CVIII

Marks have eyes / mouths / guiles / modes of touching. Where now is the in / sight they blighted with the ignorance of the wait? Between cause and effect lives an unperformed task. The disappearance clambers to places it has been / rides long-gone broncos / scandalizes logic, no theory possible. It builds neighboring houses in order to be near the name not found on the broken piece.

CVIII

Las marcas tienen ojos / boca / engaños / formas de tocar. ¿Por dónde anda la ver / dad que ajaron con ignorancias de la espera? Entre la causa y el efecto vive un trabajo sin obra. La desaparición sube a lugares donde estuvo / cabalga en potros idos / escandaliza la razón sin teoría posible. Construye casas de vecino para estar cerca del nombre que no encuentra en el pedazo roto.

CIX

Lady Flesh of the Species, merchants lopped off your wings, leaving you with no distance from your self, no land to kindle your bones in God's great zero. A purple tree is growing, with four boles, space watered by ten fountains for the sight and sound of the dagger's delicacies. Papers wrapped in fog will not suffice. The being must be told not to mate with its deceptions / sad corners / January's syllables. Who took Miguel away without his passport?

For Miguel Briante
in memoriam

CIX

Carne señora de la especie, los mercantes te quitaron el ala, te dejaron sin distancia a vos misma, sin tierra que te encienda los huesos en el cero de Dios. Crece un árbol violeta, una belleza en cuatro pies, un espacio regado por diez fuentes para vista y oído de las delicadezas del puñal. No bastan los papeles que cubre la neblina. Hay que decirle al ser que no copule con engaños de sí / rincones tristes / sílabas de enero. ¿Quién se llevó a Miguel sin pasaporte?

A Briante
in memoriam

CX

Bluebirds warp the landscape when all the world grows pale
and metaphors, anacoluthons, epanadiplosis, enallages,
pataphors, oxymora collapse and flee like the accursed
of the tongue. Where do old tatters wind up? Will they
approach someone to beg for spare change, explanations on
the street? The gaze turns to the gazing, the voice to the
speaking, the evidence mounts in ink for hire.

CX

Los pájaros azules deforman el paisaje cuando el mundo
se pone pálido y metáforas, anacolutos, epanadiplosis,
enálages, patáforas, oximorones caen y huyen como
malditos de la lengua. ¿A dónde irán harapos viejos? ¿Se
acercarán a alguno para pedir limosna, explicaciones en la
calle? La mirada se va al mirar, la voz se va al hablar, crecen
las evidencias de tintas alquiladas.

CXI

A rose sustains the world / seditious lover rising up. She won't step foot in theological fortresses, recompose the details of dismay. Unfettering herself from repetition, she prefers what is burning in a silence under siege. With each petal she pays for gloomy miseries / branchless birds / fear's submission. She creates deeds time cannot devour. She is the nation of dreams that continue to dream / all alone / heart ever true.

CXI

Una rosa sostiene al mundo / amante sublevada. No entra en fortalezas teológicas, no recompone detalles del espanto. Se desapega de la repetición, prefiere lo que arde en un silencio asediado. Con cada pétalo paga miserias tristes / los pájaros sin rama / la sumisión del miedo. Crea actos que el tiempo no se puede comer. Es la nación de sueños que sueñan todavía / sola ahí / sin falso corazón.

CXII

The delusions of disguise have faces streaked with ash.
Games with the other resemble an animal in search of a
name. Children swelter in the duration, nights that torture.
At one point in the separation, the past of the point fails
and everything falls into place. In such a fashion love will
spy on the crow eating out of its hand.

CXII

Las alucinaciones del disfraz tienen cenizas en la cara. Los
juegos con el otro se parecen a un animal que busca nombre.
Hijos sudan en la duración, las noches que torturan. En
el instante falla el pasado del instante y todo se une en la
separación. Así espía el amor al cuervo que come de su
mano.

CXIII

The animal presses on / no sound of sadness / nailed to its pain / never reined to gentle bits. It grieves at the sight of a death where longing remains moist, the antithesis of an order that fills blank pages, unpaid debts. Is this how, when exiled from things, bodies press on? The heart combines disaster and marvel, traversing the batons' shooting stars / horror inspects the oven that will preserve it.

CXIII

El animal avanza sin llanto / clavado a su dolor / no se ata a suaves frenos. Se apena por la muerte sin evaporación de los deseos, la antítesis del orden que llena hojas en blanco, las deudas sin pagar. ¿Así avanzan los cuerpos en el exilio de las cosas? El corazón combina desastre y maravilla, cruza la exhalación de los bastones / el horror revisa el horno que lo conservará.

CXIV

Does nursing someone in his madness nurse the madness? The mouth that sketches hell, does it emerge from a sacrifice returned to its ignorance? The feeble specimen blocks his pulse / shameful brain cells / threadbare posturing. Bulls surround the manger where the void was born / tongue-locked milk / insurrections of compassion. The nerves in their jail plead for a morsel more of joy / the similarity of muted and muzzled / imitations of eternity / the color of loving so much.

CXIV

Cuidar al otro en su locura, ¿es cuidar su locura? La boca que dibuja el infierno, ¿sale de un sacrificio devuelto a su ignorancia? El débil ejemplar bloquea su pulso / neuronas con vergüenza / delgada impostura. Toros rodean el pesebre donde nació el vacío / la leche lengua adentro / insurrecciones de la compasión. Los nervios en su cárcel ruegan que aumente la alegría / la semejanza de mudos y callados / imitaciones de la eternidad / el color amar tanto.

CXV

From your humiliations a flame was born / quickening beyond. Unknown your color while you ate them and ended up clearing the dishes. You float above the text like a lord / lady of spells and chainless days. You bettered Death and there you were, gibbeted to words, digging lovepits in unsaid beasts, copulating with that which is not.

For José Lezama Lima

CXV

De tus humillaciones nació un fulgor / hace vivir. Se ignora tu color cuando te las comiste y limpiaste la mesa después. Flotás fuera del texto como señor / doña de hechizos y días sin cadenas. Mejoraste a la muerte y ahí estabas, en los patíbulos de la palabra cavabas pozos de amor en las bestias no dichas, copulabas con lo que no es.

A José Lezama Lima

CXVI

Why be a tenant of the wound when the word is a woman? Erroneous lives, the calculus of desolation, enslavement of the self. Long-wandering errancy on the wings of the unconscious. Enamored she sleeps on the edge of the bed like spice on frost. Yestermint restores the slender thread of reason and anemic sightlessness. No one marries the victim, horror swallows questions, bones look beyond to minister their escape. Callow eyes fall mute in a well that collapses into its bedrock.

CXVI

¿Para qué ser inquilino de la herida si la palabra es mujer? Vidas equivocadas, cálculos de la desolación, la esclavitud de sí. La errancia larga con alas de inconsciencia. La enamorada duerme al borde de la cama como sazón del frío. Las buenayerbas devolverán los hilitos de la razón y cegueras sin sangre. Nadie se casa con la víctima, el horror come preguntas, el hueso mira afuera para cuidar su fuga. Callan los ojos sin oficio en un pozo que va a su fondo.

CXVII

Truth broils lives. Who has chanced to see it, alone in its damnation? Is death acquainted with it? Does it live there on lackluster surfaces? Uninterested in the instant? Is it awaiting mouths of beauty? Might it hold oceans and forests of unknown humanity? How does one dance to its beat? Is there ever reprieve from the misery that keeps it from speaking? In a wink it fashions faces, just in case.

CXVII

La verdad cuece vidas. ¿Quién la vio alguna vez, sola en su maldición? ¿La muerte la conoce, vive allí en superficies sin reflejo? ¿No le importa el instante? ¿Espera bocas de belleza? ¿Tiene mares y selvas de humanidad desconocida? ¿Cómo se baila a su compás? ¿Descansa alguna vez de la miseria que no la deja hablar? En un soplo cultiva rostros por si acaso.

CXVIII

Anima's light waxes and wanes like the moon. The head of
the soul is a woman avid for codices none can find in the
sage's palace / feet bleed in the burs on the road. Instinct
weeps for love's losses with due tenderness. Above / below
the forms there is a stranger / smoothing out icy beds.
World with no expectation of being, with neither greeting
nor horse to spur the authorless days.

CXVIII

La luz del ánima crece y decrece como luna. La cabeza del
alma es una mujer ávida de códices que nadie encuentra
en el palacio de los sabios / sangran pies en los abrojos del
camino. El instinto llora las pérdidas de amor con ternura
debida. Arriba / debajo de las formas hay un desconocido /
arregla lechos fríos. Mundo sin pretensión de ser, sin cosas
que saluden ni caballo espoleando los días sin autor.

CXIX

The sky's dominions have viscera like a body / the unfortunate are unaware of their love. Gunpowder's workforce hides in time's grottos, February or July, their portions. It is a grandeur preoccupied with homeless mysteries, blood's eggs, expended pyres. Embracing maleficent arts, it cradles them rocking in the pendulum of each birth. It knows of its beginning without beginning and its nights are not shattered by gloomy gods.

CXIX

Las regiones del cielo tienen entrañas como cuerpo / desdichados no conocen su amor. La mano de obra de la pólvora aguarda en las cuevas del tiempo, febrero o julio, sus porciones. Es una grandeza preocupada por los misterios que no tienen techo, los huevos de la sangre, las piras consumidas. Abraza artes malditas, las acuna en vaivenes de cada nacimiento. Sabe de su comienzo sin comienzo y dioses tristes no le rompen la noche.

CXX

The forest shades the emanations of loss / opening internal seas / we know not how to sail. Blindness shudders without a helm / hopes soaked to the bone. Between being and being-here now the vertical is raised, which joins them like a pageless book. Sorrow's prison is narrow, bathed in a pallid light as proof of light. Freedom asks when it will be invented.

CXX

El bosque da sombra a las emanaciones de la pérdida. Agranda mares interiores / no los sabemos navegar. Tiemblan cegueras sin timón / las esperas mojadas. Entre el ser y el estar se alza la vertical que los une como libro sin páginas. La prisión del dolor es estrecha, la baña una luz pálida que es prueba de la luz. La libertad pregunta cuándo la inventarán.

CXXI

Horror has riverbeds where it fails to flow. A frozen crystal mirror emerges. The intrusion of muted banks leaves deposits of the past in the depths of waiting. The tongue gleams in its dirge-filled flight / irresponsible shrieks / unhinging of the golden bed. But there they are, crestfallen, not sad from striking, but rather from that which has stricken their nakedness.

For Marco Antonio Campos

CXXI

El horror tiene cauces por donde no se va. Asoma un espejo de cristal detenido. La invasión de las orillas mudas deposita el pasado en fondos de la espera. La lengua resplandece en su fuga de quejumbres / llantos irresponsables / desquicios de la cama de oro. Pero ahí están, con la cabeza gacha, no tristes por pegar, sino por lo que pegó su desnudez.

A Marco Antonio Campos

CXXII

Slice the birds open to see what lies inside, raze the columns of the polis, the sewers of the ill-tempered miser; who can tell where one's own poisons may plume. The questions of the self have lost the innocence of former struggles, posing why the material world and the other join together to contemplate the whole of neither. The palm yet intact is still open to the back'n'forth processions, when, amid life's inventions, the I of being longed to be.

For José Nun

CXXII

Abran los pájaros a ver qué tienen, derriben las columnas de la polis, las cloacas del mísero impaciente, quién sabe dónde crecen los venenos propios. Las preguntas de sí perdieron la candidez de viejas luchas, quieren saber por qué el mundo corpóreo y el otro se juntan a contemplar el todo del ninguno. La palma intacta sigue abierta a procesiones de adelante patrás, cuando lo yo del ser quiso ser en invenciones de la vida.

A José Nun

CXXIII

On a hidden sheet of paper he scribbles the impossible / or invisible / or the marriage of the mot juste, the soirée / decryptions of the pause. Not one quill is listening / nor relative / nor liaison / merciless sky. He intercepts the not-to-be with a threatening arm and busies himself with time, faces that echo, child of an early death. He amasses the counterweights of anti-movement / suspensions left ajar. Reverberating in futile ears he makes gifts of wretched things.

CXXIII

En un papel oculto escribe el imposible / o invisible / o casamiento con la palabra justa, la fiesta / desciframientos de la pausa. No hay pluma que lo escuche / ni relación / ni enlace / su cielo sin piedad. Intercepta el no ser con brazo airado y se ocupa del tiempo, rostros que lo repiten / el niño que murió temprano. Acumula equilibrios del anti-movimiento / las suspensiones entreabiertas. Vibra sin suerte en los oídos y obsequia cosas tristes.

CXXIV

Symptoms of open spaces / counterwinds of submissions / smokescreens of double truths / thickened rhetoric. The evanescence of ties schools us in swoons that no one wants to learn and being-here wanders along with errancies between the duration and the winding down. Its reality rejects desertless doubts. Basically the questions are quite dead.

For Lucila Pagliai

CXXIV

Los síntomas del descampado / vientos contrarios de la sumisión / cortinas de humo de las dos verdades / la retórica espesa. La impermanencia de los lazos enseña deliquios que no se quieren aprender y el estar pasa con errancias entre la duración y el cese. Su realidad rechaza dudas sin desierto. En el fondo hay preguntas muy muertas.

A Lucila Pagliai

CXXV

The void abandons all conjecture. There it goes, from one body to the next, from the third turn of the metaphor to the sclerosis of the moment. It so loved the noblest truth, now on the lists of falsehoods. Chapters of being erected in shifting waters, one seal to seal it shut with yet another on top and others to make a palimpsest of illegible script. Memory breaks down in the vicissitudes of disguises, illusion-made illusions, the tongue's aged nights. They are polishing sudden fields of flax / self-distraction is a stony field.

For Antonio Cisneros
In memoriam

CXXV

El vacío abandona todas las conjeturas. Ahí va, de un cuerpo a otro, de la tercera vez de la metáfora a la esclerosis del instante. Tanto quería la verdad más noble, ahora en las listas de lo falso. Se construyen capítulos del ser en aguas que se mueven, lo sella un sello y otro encima y otros más hacen un palimpsesto con escrituras ilegibles. La memoria se rompe en peripecias del disfraz, las ilusiones que producen ilusión, las noches viejas de la lengua. Pulen linares repentinos mientras la distracción de sí es un campo yerto.

A Antonio Cisneros
In memoriam

CXXVI

Legs lost in the passions of the landscape, sentences of totality, writs of the ibis. The rain's assistants fracture the copper and moisten the questions / loaves of bread brought to their knees. One search collapses and from it begin to sprout gardenias / belated / perfuming what was headed for the wind and got stuck on the ground. Words that tremble in its muck bloom in latitudes of difficulty, their black and white go in and out of the self to target the other in a compass unfit for circles. And so much life outside, so much life wrapped in the flame of a fallen verb.

CXXVI

Pies perdidos en las pasiones del paisaje, sentencias de la totalidad, papeles de la garza. Los ayudantes de la lluvia rompen el cobre y mojan las preguntas / los panes de rodillas. Cayó una búsqueda y le crecen gardenias / tarde / aroman lo que iba al viento y quedó en tierra. Palabras que tiemblan en su lodo se abren en latitudes de la dificultad, su negro blanco entra y sale del yo al otro en un compás que no sabe trazar círculos. Y tanta vida afuera, tanta vida envuelta en el fulgor de un verbo cáido.

CXXVII

What does saying know about not saying? Does it drown
its seedlings, run from its design? The interns on the other
side of the mirror parley as if they were on the far side of
language. The heart sets sail on ships that may sink and
alcohol seeps into the liver of the Verb. On its underbelly
there are other bodies, surfaces of inherited grief, freedoms
that deny the abyss and clamber up a hilltop that cannot
be pronounced. Spacious enough for each and all, though
tainted by their lot.

CXXVII

¿Qué sabe el decir del no decir? ¿Ahoga sus plantitas, huye
de su trazado? Los practicantes de fuera del espejo parlan
como si fueran otros del lenguaje. El corazón se embarca en
naves que se pueden hundir y el alcohol entra el hígado del
Verbo. En su envés hay otros cuerpos, superficies de penas
heredadas, libertades que niegan el abismo y suben una
cuesta que no se puede pronunciar. Tiene espacios donde
todos cabrían ya impuros de su suerte.

CXXVIII

Do not sully the day when all is seen through love. The depiction of the three stones refutes the lifeless wit of explanations, the traces of allusions, lofty philosophical summits. It speaks of paradises, each unique, and of vulgar, platonic hells we tailor for ourselves like custom-made suits. The bond between these territories is a slender thread that marks the span between being and being here, two strangers that look at each other without understanding and stand in adoration of their distance. Autumn's wind chills the bones of the union / it resembles a cozened goldfinch.

CXXVIII

Que nadie dañe el día en que todo se mira por amor. La representación de las tres piedras niega la sal muertita de las explicaciones, los signos de las referencias, las altas cumbres filosóficas. Habla de paraísos que en nada se parecen y de infiernos vulgares y platónicos que cada quien se cose como un traje. El lazo de estos territorios es un hilito que marca la distancia entre el ser y el estar, dos extraños que se miran sin comprender y aman su lejanía. El viento del otoño enfría huesos de la unidad / se parece a un jilguero traicionado.

CXXIX

Things so concealed in selfness befall the world. Inhabitants of the marrow experience the affair on a pokey little burro. Pure outside does not exist / center / palmtrees to protect from distraction. The relation between blindness and the power of blindness is a poorly-fastened rope that winter compels us to comprehend. In the dissimilarities of gunshots, tomorrow's boldness stumbles.

CXXIX

Pasan cosas de mucho secreto en el sí mismo al mundo. Los habitantes de la entraña viven el acto en un burrito lento. No hay fueras puras / centro / palmares que protejan de la distracción. La relación entre lo ciego y la fuerza de lo ciego es una cuerda mal tendida que el invierno obliga a comprender. En las desemejanzas de los tiros cae el atrevimiento de mañana.

CXXX

Spies of the commonplace discover drifting labyrinths / the fiat soul of the underside / the coordinates of holding out / the obscure table where a hyacinth died. That which is structured falls apart and only they take note. Ten different names for the rain filter through the clefts of a carnation / restitching the seams of the trodden soil by means of the trodden self.

CXXX

Los espías de lo común encuentran un laberinto a la deriva / el haga alma de un envés / las coordenadas del aguante / la mesa apagada donde murió un jacinto. Lo estructurado se deshace y sólo ellos se dan cuenta. Por las hendijas de un clavel caen diez nombres de la lluvia / recosen las suturas del pisar la tierra con el pisado de sí mismo.

CXXXI

When permitted to speak does experience begin to wither?
The afterward given voice end in betrayal? What becomes
of it, where, when? Does it find furies spanning centuries /
do they feed on time? Suns of long-gone notions? The not
to be of love so it may be? The river that ran with hands
enclasped? A child engrossed in his childhood? Places where
goodness incubates evil? The slouching wings of a silent
piety? The cold trembles at bygone doors that bang again
and again.

For Teresa Franco

CXXXI

¿Se amustia lo vivido cuando le dan palabra? ¿El después
hablado lo traiciona? ¿Y qué le hace, dónde, cómo?
¿Encuentra viejas furias que atravesaron siglos / comen
tiempo? ¿Soles de ideas idas? ¿El no ser del amor para que
sea? ¿El río que pasaba con las manos juntas? ¿Un niño
absorto en su niñez? ¿Lugares donde el bien incuba el mal?
¿Las alas gachas de una piedad muda? El frío tiembla en
puertas del pasado que vuelven a golpear.

A Teresa Franco

CXXXII

Medicine cannot explain why a woman's gaze spatters red on what she sees. Is there a name for that? The day gone by puts insanity to bed in separations of the tongue and biennial marriages that never file for divorce. Were you trounced? Fine. Did you win? Fine. Within your roots live the prehistory of partial love, the diamond that dimmed, the impracticalities of signing the death certificate of haunted nights. The reflection of oneself is a sad companion. Here and there the heavens fling tatters of desire and disparities of a thing / though it may live in the marsh and know it must die.

CXXXII

La ciencia médica no explica por qué la mirada de una mujer salpica de rojo lo que mira. ¿Qué nombre tiene eso? El día que pasó acuesta a la locura en separaciones de la lengua y matrimonios del bienal que nunca se divorcian. ¿Te derrotaron?, bien. ¿Ganaste?, bien. En tu raíz viven la prehistoria del amor parcial, el diamante que apágase, imposibilidades de firmar el certificado de muerte de noches poseídas. La reflexión de sí es un compañero triste. Cielos tiran de aquí para allá harapos de las improporciones y el deseo de una cosa / aunque viva en un pantano y sepa que ha de morir.

CXXXIII

Reclining in a chair provides a better view of the destruction of a hummingbird. Lounging in its death, color still sings, remembering the oblique line of flight. Now resting in its short-lived beauty, it penetrates the depths consummated by the desire to embrace the countlessness of humanity's ensemble, to step on the nape of sorrow so news of the joy might arrive. Hummingbird that disappears into dry leaves and a darkened me.

CXXXIII

Descansar en una silla permite ver mejor la destrucción de un colibrí. Acostado en su muerte, el color canta todavía, recuerda la línea oblicua del pasar. Ya quieto en su belleza que poco durará / entra en profundidades consumadas por el deseo de abrazar al sinfín humano entero, pisar la nuca del dolor para que lleguen informaciones de la dicha. Colibrí que te vas en hojas secas y un yo oscuro.

CXXXIV

That which breaks free of order's disorder is clandestine, finding refuge in the law of gravity. It wanders in sleepwalking kinships that demand God's sarcophagus be closed, launching flights from itself to its own ignorance with no other shelter than nakedness. This act is a havenless sea one must navigate amid lessons of poverty, mutilations of the spirit, the indefatigable maestro of repetition.

CXXXIV

Lo que escapa del desorden del orden es clandestino, se refugia en la ley de gravedad. Anda en sangres sonámbulas que exigen que se cierre el sarcófago de Dios, se alcen vuelos de sí a la propia ignorancia sin otro abrigo que la desprotección. Este acto tiene mares sin puertos a navegar entre lecciones de pobreza, mutilaciones del espíritu, el mester incansable de la repetición.

CXXXV

Sadness fell silent whenever he passed by and the tailors of wretchedness would flee. He entered what none dare enter, informed and fearless he donned love's tatters, strolling nocturnal streets where celebration rhymes with loneliness and with bodies in defiance of infectious servitude. In the spoils of grace he placed his solemnly-swear that burns in times of truth. He castigated human dispassion and cultivated lips for the goldfinch. With God he raised a glass so He might recognize the vacuities of speech / enigmas in the floss where poetry nests. In such radiance he confers feasible meetings, freedom's incertitudes, the compassion of the imagination.

For Mario Trejo
In memoriam

CXXXV

Enmudecía la tristeza cuando pasaba él y los sastres de la mezquindad huían. Entró en lo que nadie entra. Supo y vistió sin miedo harapos del amor, calles nocturnas en que celebración rima con soledad y cuerpo rebelde a servidumbres contagiosas. En los despojos de la gracia puso su sí que arde en tiempos verdaderos. Castigó la despasión humana y cultivó los labios del jilguero. Brindó con Dios para que reconozca vacíos en la lengua / enigmas en los hilos donde la poesía se acuesta. En su fulgor deja encuentros posibles, incertidumbres de la libertad, compasiones de la imaginación.

A Mario Trejo
in memoriam

CXXXVI

An entourage of beggars files by soliciting approval. The custom of labeling muddies the image. Poverty hunkers down in delirium's conformation, and the secretaries of things inoculate the crazed. The political machine crushes every province of the spirit. Death pays it a call in the *arrabales* of the self while lofty fires ask what a father is and snuff themselves out the moment they begin to hear.

CXXXVI

Un cortejo de mendigos pasa pidiendo aprobación. La costumbre de etiquetar ensucia imágenes. La pobreza se instala en la estructura del delirio y ministros de las cosas vacunan a los locos. La máquina política aplasta provincias del espíritu. Se muere en arrabales de sí mismo, altos fuegos preguntan qué es un padre y se apagan cuando empiezan a oír.

CXXXVII

When reason turns tender, autumn will cease to shed its leaves.
They will become conundrums of being / yellow / useless /
blind to their mother's face / delusions of things. They need
to see, taste, hear, touch a dog, listen to their passion, leave
the ruins of writing behind. The will's tension dances in the
square meters of time. In such a fashion there once bloomed
a flower the centuries cannot touch / love sweats.

For Víctor Sandoval
In memoriam

CXXXVII

Cuando la razón sea sensible el otoño no tirará sus hojas.
Serán incógnitas del ser / amarillas / inútiles / no verán el
rostro de su madre / las alucinaciones de las cosas. Necesitan
oído, gusto, ver, tocar un perro, escuchar su pasión, dejar
atrás ruinas de la escritura. En los metros cuadrados del
tiempo danzan tensiones de la voluntad. Así nació una flor
que los siglos no pueden tocar / el amor suda.

A Víctor Sandoval
In memoriam

CXXXVIII

When eternal exaltedness flies like a blind planet in one's head, the heart defends itself in a room full of mad beasts. Who knows more of incandescence? Relations with human cheeks are the found amid the lost. The cosmic clock plunges, the vertigo of consciousness is the improbable source of the other, substance herded on by exile.

CXXXVIII

Cuando lo altísimo increado vuela como planeta ciego en la cabeza, el corazón se defiende en un cuarto con animales locos. ¿Quién sabe más de incandescencias? Las relaciones con mejillas humanas son el hallado en el perdido. El reloj cósmico se abaja, el vértigo de la conciencia es la fuente improbable del otro, substancia arreada por exilios.

CXXXIX

Blood's rage trudges across fields of nothing's going on. The spirit's temperature dropped during occasions of the species and the theoretical arsenal of its invention lies in tatters. Where is the quake of body and soul? In the circumference of consciousness lies defeat / plots of imitation / servitudes that reek. World that might have been and might not have believed that one word is the same as any other.

CXXXIX

La furia de una sangre atraviesa los campos del no pasa nada. Bajó la temperatura del espíritu en ocasiones de la especie y el arsenal teórico de su invención es puro trapo. ¿A dónde fue el temblor en cuerpo y alma? En los perímetros de la conciencia hay derrotas / tramas de la imitación / servidumbres que apestan. Mundo que fueses y no creyeras que una palabra es como cualquier otra.

CXL

The strategy of constructing oneself contains the poison of acquiescence. The price / spark in the lower heart / with neither labial creatures nor identity cards. The reorganization of the mirrors yields three or four of one all separate. One? Of what? In what district? What song of the flesh can they ensemble? Uncontemplated, they don't even seek each other out. They fast in the cruelties of representation.

For Teresa Franco

CXL

La estrategia de construir el yo es un veneno del asentimiento. El precio / chispa del corazón de abajo / sin criaturas labiales ni cédulas de identidad. La reorganización de los espejos trae los tres o cuatro de uno separados. ¿Uno? ¿De qué? ¿En cuál distrito? ¿Qué canción de la carne cantan juntos? Descontemplados, ni se buscan. Ayunan en crueldades de la representación.

A Teresa Franco

CXLI

What have become of those luxuries of the landscape / kin to all and to nothing at all / life and death of the bull / tears within the brain? The ultimate difference blindly sang in its own evaporation as if in hiding, its eye interchangeable with doctrinarian tricks. The sacrifice was cheap, writing letters that burn in silence. The forbidden read them, their furies exposed, birds now beakless, roses detained in what never came.

For Juan Marsé

CXLI

¿A dónde se fueron extravagancias del paisaje / parientes del todo y de la nada / vida y muerte del toro / lágrimas en el cerebro? La diferencia última cantaba ciega en la evaporación del sí como ocultarse y el ojo intercambiable con trampas de doctrina. El sacrificio era barato y escribió cartas que arden en silencio. Las leen los prohibidos, sus furias sin amparo, aves sin pico, rosas detenidas en lo que no vinió.

A Juan Marsé

CXLII

What is gone is gone, but has left its gone. There are new suns in the wheel of constellations and desire knows only how to craft its own void. Impulse is the beginning and the end of its root and imagination crafts consolations. Briefly they appear in the mien of reality, the might-be's of sacrifice, the quiet sod at the foot of an actual bird. A chirp of grace drives them off, memory that continues to nurture.

For Rodolfo Alonso

CXLII

Lo que se fue, se fue, pero deja su fue. Hay soles nuevos en la rueda de las constelaciones y el deseo sólo sabe crear su vacío. El impulso es el comienzo y el fin de su raíz y la imaginación crea consuelos. Poco duran en apariencias de la realidad, los puede ser del sacrificio, el suelo quieto al pie de un ave verdadera. Los aleja un silbido de la gracia, la memoria que sigue dando de comer.

A Rodolfo Alonso

CXLIII

In the dread of death death isn't worth the while. The bereaved are of no interest, nor the love-maimed, nor a summer's marvelous wit. What matters is the light received in the form of entrails in which one sees oneself. The sensation of the body meeting its end does not live in a padlocked niche, it creates its double in impalpable seasons and the unnotarized aliquots of pain. A mockingbird tidies up the failure of a snuffed-out match.

CXLIII

En el miedo a la muerte la muerte no vale la pena. Los afligidos no interesan, ni los tullidos por amor, ni el portentoso ingenio de un verano. Importa la luz recibida en forma de entrañas para verse. La sensación del cuerpo que termina no vive en un rincón cerrado, crea su doble en estaciones impalpables y las alícuotas de pena sin notario. Una calandria ordena el fracaso de un fósforo apagado.

CXLIV

That which is accessible has a verso that madness pleats. Anchored ships sail through. The spine's morality is a marsh of evasion and deafness. What is there to flee if not malice? In some nameless place await the amenities of love, the duration pauses cannot yoke, what remains to be done. The thing outside the thing proposes journeys of the tongue to its long-sought oration.

CXLIV

Lo accesible tiene un envés que la locura plisa. Lo surcan naves ancladas. La moral de la espalda es un pantano de huidas y sorderas. ¿De qué se escapa sino de la ruindad? En un lugar sin nombre esperan servicios del amor, la duración que el cese no esclaviza, lo que está por hacer. La cosa fuera de la cosa propone viajes de la lengua a su oración buscada.

CXLU

Unbind me, wines that I have drunk, the trips I have taken to myself, parks where my youth got laid. The peddling of the self in illusions of the illusion, the use of courage, the hope by will alone invented. How can you not hear the rifle rounds of poverty and hunger? In averting your eyes the spirit lessens its vertigo, losing its edge, departing for the smoky speech of what has been done. Solitude pierced by the sun's leavings. There once were philosophies of invention / human meadows / souls yet unwritten / wisps of smoke unallied.

CXLU

Desátenme los vinos que bebí, los viajes a mí que hice, los parques donde cogió mi juventud. El mercadeo del ser en ilusiones de la ilusión, empleos del coraje, la esperanza inventada a voluntad. ¿Cómo no oír los tiros de la pobreza y del hambre? En no mirar por nada el espíritu achica su mareo, pierde el filo, se va al discurso ahumado de lo hecho. Soledad agujereada por las sobras del sol. Había filosofías del invento / campos humanos / almas no escritas todavía / humean sin aliados.

CXLVI

The word eucalyptus, childhood patios, their infatuations
are victories for Archilochus, Catullus, Ovid, John Donne,
who slumbering next to his impending tomb said, *love
forges alchemies.* The nightingale trills its tune bearing
bones fretted by endless frost. But Alcman is present, with
his *breast of forest night* and passion, Catullus countering
Caesar. The Calends of May left Raimbaut de Vaqueiras
dismayed, repeating themselves and posing questions,
serfs of good and evil, the puncture of failed dreams, the
opposite day of the inimical yes. Our gratitude, Sappho, for
a tongue free of evil affairs. Swift rivers of the skin confirm
your affable bond with golden beasts.

CXLVI

La palabra eucaliptus, los patios de la infancia, sus amores
fugaces, son victorias de Arquíloco, Catulo, Ovidio, John
Donne que dormía en su próximo ataúd dijo *amor fragua
alquimias.* El ruiseñor modula su cantar y tiene huesos
calados por frío fijos. Pero está Alcmán, el de la *noche bosque
del pecho* y la pasión, Catulo contra el César. Las calendas
de mayo entristecían a Raimbaut de Vaqueiras, se repiten
y hacen preguntas, inquilinas del bien y el mal, la punción
de sueños fracasados, el día opuesto al sí enemigo. Gracias,
Safo, por no tener la lengua en cosa mala. Ríos veloces de la
piel confirman tu amistad con bestias de oro.

CXLVII

There are Pampas where free of bridle and bit the furies gallop wherever their fancy leads. Systems of servitude cannot bate them, they disturb the classical universe. The irresponsibility of the imagination reworks its senses and established thought. They have sun-born egrets that deposit plumes free of interest in an open wound.

CXLVII

Hay pampas donde furias sin brida ni trinquete galopan a su antojo. Sistemas de la servidumbre no pueden apagarlas, desordenan el universo clásico. Las inconsciencias de la imaginación trabajan sus sentidos y la razón sentada. Tienen garzas del sol que depositan sin intereses plumas en una herida.

CXLVIII

In tatters, in tuxedos, in all forms of nudity, she looks at an open hand as if the implacable would ever spare a dime. Goddess with no recognizable children, she protects her nonbeing on human turf. She's the little girl lost in unwashed mouths. The resignation of the nonword word, she travels between upper and lower voices, scandals where life has no worth.

For Marifé Santiago

CXLVIII

Con harapos, con frac, con muy desnuda, mira una mano abierta como si la implacable fuera capaz de dar limosna. Diosa sin hijos conocidos, protege su no ser en campo humano. Es la niña perdida en bocas mal lavadas. La resignación de la palabra no palabra, viaja entre voces de arriba y las de abajo, escándalos donde la vida vale nada.

A Marifé Santiago

CXLIX

Who is it that corrects the word piece / its limits / separations / its flight of roots? Where now is the hand that orchestrated their gazes? The pieces of self no longer ensemble in song / versions of that oneness / the shade of clouds. Foregone the parties where reason raised a glass to the arithmetic of the lip. In a seat of honor, legitimate beasts wield reality without so much as a warning.

CXLIX

¿Quién corrige la palabra pedazo / sus límites / separaciones / su vuelo de raíces? ¿Dónde quedó la mano que unía sus miradas? Los pedazos de sí ya no tienen músicas juntas / versiones de la unidad / la sombra de las nubes. Se acabaron las fiestas donde la razón brindaba por matemáticas del labio. En un puesto de honor, bestias legítimas usan la realidad sin advertencias.

CL

The bud the bud, the bud, the blooming, mute within my hand. Useless to weep for the dead / she says / useless to weep for the living / she says / then grows a little bluer. In the corners of a straight line there are hollows where semiotics lapse. The visible that is here / the invisible that is here / stirring good and evil in a potpourri. A purple sea of separations becomes a void the sparrows never visit. Nothing is eaten there / the only flight, impossibility with its heavy tremor.

CL

La flor la flor, la flor, la florida, muda en mi mano. Es inútil llorar por los muertos / dice / es inútil llorar por los vivos / dice / se vuelve más azul. En los rincones de la línea recta hay cuevas donde caduca la semiótica. Lo visible que está / lo invisible que está / revuelven el bien y el mal en una olla podrida. Que un mar púrpura instale su separación es un vacío que los gorriones no visitan. Nada se come ahí, sólo vuela la imposibilidad con un temblor espeso.

CLI

Long days level the names of belonging. To what / to whom / to which beds? Do they bleed when they discover their destiny? The ink that mixed the line of rhythmic functions changed the folds of its music, eye-locked tongue, ancient theories of the self. Local passions cannot see things as they are. The word inspectors know nothing of the price of courage, its mistakes, its mysteries in a golden box. Nerval's star-filled lute falls silent for the passengers of paucity.

CLI

Los días largos talan nombres de la pertenencia. ¿A qué / a quiénes / a qué lechos? ¿Sangran cuando conocen su destino? La tinta que cruzó funciones rítmicas cambió los pliegues de su música, la lengua de ojo adentro, viejas teorías del yo mismo. Pasiones regionales no ven las cosas como son. Los inspectores de la palabra ignoran el precio del coraje, sus equivocaciones, sus misterios en una caja de oro. El laúd constelado de Nerval enmudece para los pasajeros de lo poco.

CLII

Treatises are written to explain everything except why that is not that. Poetry is not that, the purple hatred is not that, living / dying, not that. The meeting between the attraction and its repulsion founds cities where both of them weep. What is it about the nonbeing of the being? The poplar that props up the soul? Clinics for the void, beggars of the not other, looking into the eyes of the I, which inescapably leaves a lack? A tree takes its own life, the rain cleanses fanciful fugues.

CLII

Escriben tratados que explican todo menos por qué eso no es eso. La poesía no es eso, el odio púrpura no es eso, vivir / morir no es eso. El encuentro de la atracción con su repulsa funda ciudades donde lloran. ¿Qué habrá en lo no ser del ser? ¿Un álamo que se alma? ¿Clínicas del vacío, mendigos del no otro, verse que hace la falta sin remedio? Un árbol se suicida, la lluvia lava fugas de la imaginación.

CLIII

The agony of the hummingbird gleamed like a gem. Sparks from her flight, her slight, her disguise, the third person singular of death, briefly beneath the moon. How lengthy her leaving. The candescence of the instant transformed a darkened earth into a vigil of ashes. She used to wonder where the word would glide while canvassing mankind.

CLIII

La agonía del colibrí brillaba como joya. Destellos de su vuelo, su desazón, su máscara, la tercera persona de la muerte, breves bajo la luna. Qué lento fue su irse. La incandescencia del instante cambió la tierra oscura en una vigilia de cenizas. Solía preguntarse a dónde iba la flotación de la palabra en su rastreo humano.

CLIV

Will this river never end? Who is feeding it? Does it bind and gag recollections looking to flee? The letters leave the matter in senseless names. The edges of the spiral in motion have a thousand eyes / limpets stuck to the wound. The links between the lap-winged *teros* and the air form hollows free of hospital stench, and in a firewine lie one hundred years written to counter wrinkled repetitions. Memory arrives with what's missing from the is / mirror beyond repair.

CLIV

¿Por qué este río no se acaba? ¿Quién le da de comer? ¿Maniata recuerdos que se quieren ir? El signo deja la cosa en nombres sin sentido. Los costados de la espiral en movimiento tienen mil ojos / lapas pegadas a la herida. Los vínculos del tero con el aire hacen cuevas sin olor a hospital y en un vino de fuego hay cien años escritos contra repeticiones arrugadas. La memoria viene con lo ido en el es / espejo sin arreglo.

CLU

Squeeze the secrets of being here to see if any juice is left, love, love, icicles and laces of com/passion. Country the sorrow, decrypt the wide ribbons of punishment, fall not asleep at the foot of the stonings. World that prods with warblood, you will never master your poetry, it treats the wrong cancer.

CLU

Retuerzan los entresijos del estar a ver si dan jugo todavía, amor, amor, carámbanos y telas de la com/pasión. Paísen sufrimientos, descifren las anchas cintas del castigo, no se duerman al pie de las pedradas. Mundo que insistís con sangres de la guerra, nunca dominarás a tu poesía, te opera el cáncer indebido.

CLUI

Hokum's jitters kill crows. Grab onto the presage, the imputable names, the cozy home of yesteryear, the slayer of servitudes. May the physical clarity of the bottle come to moisten the disasters with its bonding secret.

CLUI

El repelús de la candonga mata cuervos. Agarrate al presagio, los nombres imputables, la casita que fue, el matadón de servidumbres. Que venga el claro físico de la botella a mojar los desastres con su secreto que une.

CLVII

Blood twists his arm in his tired times. An obstinate yesterday barges in / shorn of himself he gazes at a mirror inured to defeat / lives in the rhythm of eyelids oblivious to the day. Between the natural and the fictitious person he tends the syntax he loved, inflection's broncos / understanding that in paltry spaces there's room for the marvel of the dog that always tags along.

CLVII

La sangre le dobla el brazo a sus veces cansadas. Está solo de sí / el ayer obstinado lo interrumpe. Se mira en un espejo acostumbrado a la derrota. Vive el ritmo de párpados ignorantes del día. Entre la persona natural y la ficticia cuida sintaxis que amó, los potros del acento. Entendió que en espacios mezquinos cabe la maravilla del perro que te sigue.

CLVIII

The responsibility of the dream is an act. Yesterday tomorrow writes its vowels so time might last. What will become of this obedience? How much fits into a word? Preserving machines, recklessness. Rhythm organizes its loss in stellar distractions, drifting in childhood sadness, marking the pain and joy of glimpsing the eyes of a deer.

CLVIII

La responsabilidad del sueño es un acto. Ayer mañana escribe sus vocales para que el tiempo dure. ¿A dónde va a parar esta obediencia? ¿Cuánto cabe en una palabra? Preservación de máquinas, descuidos. El ritmo organiza su pérdida en distracciones estelares, vaga en tristezas de la infancia, marca las penas y los goces de la mirada a un ciervo.

CLIX

The poem passes from the real to experience / to imagination / to a word far from its cradle / bereft of the fires of the mother's plumpness. What country is it bound for on crutches? Leaving rich and poor in moldy leaves / trembling in unison / moments that found no river / fervor with no filiation / the I dry and wry / silences of its calcination, one hard chunk among the ashes / night that begins to buck.

For Geneviève Fabry

CLIX

El poema pasa del real a la vivencia / a la imaginación / a una palabra lejos de su cuna / sin fuegos de la rotunda madre. ¿A qué país se va en muletas? En hojas mustias deja a ricos y pobres / temblaron por igual / instantes que no encontraron río / fulgor sin filiación / el yo seco / silencios de su calcinación con un pedazo duro en las cenizas / corcovo de la noche.

A Geneviève Fabry

CLX

The elements have a knack for making adversity flow. Its animals are grazing in the distances contained within the self, compelling it to tell the truth. The erudite populace doesn't ponder the banishment of the heart, the castigated nape, the peak of its potential. They live in volumes of tangible virtue, the certitude of gravity, the treatment of the insane, walls of explanation opposite the starving.

CLX

La facultad de la intemperie hace fluir desdichas. En las distancias de uno mismo comen sus animales para que diga la verdad. Las poblaciones eruditas no piensan en destierros del corazón, la nuca castigada, el más de su posible. Viven en libros de virtudes tangibles, la certidumbre de la gravedad, el tratamiento de los locos, muros de la explicación en sentido contrario al muerto de hambre.

CLXI

There is a sea we blindly sail / without communions for its cleansing. Its nakedness collides with famous burials of the tongue / dispassion standing tall. The nobody is nothing, Augustine, *the tabernacles shelter the rich not the poor, the weak, the world's obscure.* They close the mouths of the mindful and theory murders forests. Once upon a time the moon lay in rivers she now visits with the accents of a name yet to come / her plausible mask.

CLXI

Hay un mar que navegamos ciegos / sin comuniones que lo limpien. Su desnudez topa con célebres entierros de la lengua / la despasión erguida. El nadie es nada, Agustín, *los tabernáculos abrigan a los ricos no a pobres, los débiles, los oscuros del mundo.* Cierran la boca del atento y la teoría mata bosques. Estábase la luna en ríos que frecuenta con acentos de un nombre por venir / su máscara posible.

CLXII

Love pondering its obstacles, the distance between being and being-here now, the creatures of its steadfast moistness. The unshaped of the shapes aspires to signs of delight. The rules of chance admit neither apologies nor scattered syllables. Omens of the hunter's death distance the body from the word untouched / word seized the day the dates begin to weep.

CLXII

Amor que piensa en sus obstáculos, las distancias del ser a estar, las criaturas de su humedad intacta. Lo informe de las formas aspira a indicios del deleite. Las reglas del azar no permiten disculpas ni sílabas dispersas. Presagios de la muerte del cazador crean la ajenidad del cuerpo a la palabra sin tocar, la apresada algún día cuando las fechas lloren.

CLXIII

May the hours of the day be traded for the delinquencies
of the times, such as loving, loving, such as love. The body
clambers up the boulders of the event / behind / far off /
the cursor's fetishes / the no-lived / the cowardly scapula /
wicker prisons / versions of the dread.

CLXIII

Que se troquen las horas del día por delincuencias de la
época como amar, amar, como amar. El cuerpo trepa rocas
del acontecimiento / atrás / lejos / fetiches del cursor /
lo invivido / la escápula cobarde / cárceles de canastilla /
versiones del espanto.

CLXIV

Are the faces of love all one and the same / unicity hindering their wandering ways? What joins them if not their hereafter? The outside batters self-ignorance / denials float in recollection / truth saddens reason's central committee.

CLXIV

¿Las caras del amor son una sola / la juntidad impide su divagación? ¿Qué las une sino su más allá? El afuera golpea ignorancias de sí / en la memoria flota lo negado / la verdad entristece al comité central de la razón.

CLXV

The solution to ambiguities is others. Are the oohs born of cultivated pain? Does experience ooh within the word? What lay in the day before / hand? The vassalage of causalities cinches knots that bind the bond itself. They resist flowers / carnations / roses / flight-bound fugues of transcendence. A beak pecks at mute beasts, dried blood that ruins the past. Mockingbirds soar in the grandmother who knits nights free of surprise, partisans of her desire.

CLXV

La solución de ambigüedades es otras. ¿Los ayes nacen del dolor cultivado? ¿La experiencia ayea en la palabra? ¿Qué hubo en el día de ante / mano? El vasallaje de las causalidades sella nudos que atan al propio vínculo. Resisten flores / claveles / rosas / fugas de la trascendencia. Un pico escarba bestias mudas, sangres secas que arruinan el pasado. Calandrias vuelan en la abuela que teje noches sin asombro, huestes de su deseo.

CLXVI

The perfection of the circle does not explain the spiral, ever higher in its versions / it admits neither enclosure nor tremors of a self in danger of itself. The winds of the times cannot make it swerve from its ignorance, its sudden flame, its power divided into two incurable conflicts within the nonexistent poem.

CLXVI

La perfección del círculo no explica a la espiral, cada vez más alta en sus versiones / no admite encierros ni temblores del yo en peligro de sí mismo. Los vientos de la época no la consiguen desviar de su ignorancia, su llama repentina, su poder dividido en dos conflictos sin cura en el poema que no existe.

CLXVII

Skepticism / the driest season of resignation. Does it help to sidestep the slavery of days never to break? Is it aware that God was hurled down to his dull creatures? That to return from the dream you must bleed? In the lowlands, the tongue's abode will not suffice. The beginning has no infinity.

For Fran Sevilla

CLXVII

Escepticismo / la estación más seca de la resignación. ¿Evita servidumbres de los días que no se asomarán? ¿Sabe que Dios fue arrojado a su criatura alguna? ¿Que volver del sueño cuesta sangre? En la región de abajo no basta el domicilio de la lengua. El comienzo no tiene infinito.

A Fran Sevilla

CLXVIII

Rights grow old in their impossibility. Not even love has the right to be anything other than love / slight in times of attack. Muddled trysts drive blind doves asunder / herbs that dried long before birth / homeless ashes.

CLXVIII

Los derechos envejecen en su imposibilidad. Ni el amor tiene derecho a ser otra cosa que amor / chico en tiempos que lo atacan. El desencuentro abre palomas ciegas / hierbas que se secaron muy antes de nacer / las cenizas sin casa.

CLXIX

Comprehension brings wretched streets wrapped in fine feelings. Where are they now those adventures of splendor, late-night milongas, parleys with the body? And you, world, do you believe yourself to be flat like the pampas galloped for joyous pleasure? Being's abyss is nothing in the misfortune of being-here now. Killing off the wounds of love with love leaves love insolvent. Its essence, a blazing chunk of unhammered iron.

CLXIX

El entender trae calles con miserias envueltas en buenos sentimientos. ¿A dónde fuéronse aventuras del resplandor, milongas de la noche, correspondencias con el cuerpo? Y usted, mundo, ¿se cree plano como pampa galopada por los finos deleites? Los abismos del ser son nada en la desgracia de estar. Matar las llagas del amor con amor deja sin bienes al amor. Lo que es en sí parece un fierro ardiente no golpeado.

CLXX

Pollen seeps into hospitals, hovering over heads, filthy sheets, that one and that one over there. What could they want to eat that he himself did not eat with those final caps? Their fingers are not searching for an alternate key to blue heaven, their blood is clogged from being-here and being-here now again. The ship sets sail laden with battered steps and stupefaction.

CLXX

El polen entra en los hospitales, sobrevuela cabezas, sábanas sucias, aquél, aquél. ¿Qué querrán comer que él mismo no se comió con cápsulas finales? Sus dedos no buscan la llave alterna al cielo azul, tiene sangre tapada por el estar y estar. Se va la nave cargada de pasos golpeados y estupor.

CLXXI

In the lessons on limits, the tea from the samovar, the silences of the father, the amen of the Fridays are all of weighty consequence. The mother's repetitions persist. The journey's freedom was left behind / of its own volition the sky protects.

CLXXI

En el aprendizaje de los límites pesan el té del samovar, los silencios del padre, el amén de los viernes. Insisten repeticiones de la madre. La libertad del viaje quedó atrás / el cielo abriga sin pedir.

CLXXII

Every window or river, every skin eaten by time, every rapt desert, every teardrop in your mouth creates subterranean havens with the vision of fifteen hawks. Where will they fly if not to the tragedy no one can apprise? What is this distance with things? Does each have its private universe, embraces as figures of southern winds or flows of wreathing smoke? Secrets where a tiger is possible? In scatterings of the real Orpheus lie pages of equivocation, music of love broken, breasts that will never shine. Retired words work their roads in the being here that hides their roads in turn.

For Eduardo Lizalde

CLXXII

Cada ventana o río, cada piel que el tiempo come, cada desierto absorto, cada lágrima en la boca, crea refugios subterráneos con la visión de quince águilas. ¿A dónde volarán sino al drama que nadie sabe conocer? ¿Qué es esta distancia con las cosas? ¿Cada una tiene universo propio, abrazos en representación del viento sur o mareas del humo blandido? ¿Secretos donde un tigre es posible? En dispersiones del verdadero Orfeo descansan páginas de la equivocación, músicas del amor roto, pechos que nunca alumbrarán. Palabras retiradas trabajan su camino en el estar que oculta su camino.

A Eduardo Lizalde

CLXXIII

Yesterday's clothing sings when donned by a child. Transmission is a dark canal that dissipates in innocent bodies. Day breaks from night but how? The passenger without passage pours ruins in altered rhythms and caesuras that overcome the silence. The qualms of explication disappear in new ancient dreams of luck and the marrow of the dawn.

For Iván

CLXXIII

La ropa del pasado canta cuando la viste un niño. La transmisión es un canal oscuro que se disipa en cuerpos inocentes. ¿La aurora se separa de la noche cómo? El pasajero sin pasaje vuelca ruinas en ritmos alterados y cesuras que ganan su silencio. Hesitaciones de la explicación desaparecen en viejos sueños nuevos del azar y médulas del alba.

A Iván

CLXXIV

Those that contemplate beauty know about the stroke, the word, the B-flat that comes on a whim. What coaxed them to bestial substitution / sullied with signs left by the death of a sparrow? Alone there, on the sidewalk that did not say get a move on, flesh / up and at 'em / away away. Differences of sameness work in the repetitions of silence. Light combats the darkness it carries within.

For Jorge Boccanera

CLXXIV

Los que contemplan la hermosura saben del trazo, la palabra, el sí bemol que viene porque quiere. ¿Qué los llamó a la sustitución del animal / sucio de signos que le impuso la muerte de un gorrión? Solo ahí, en la vereda que no le dijo arriba, carne, arriba / vuela / vuela. En las repeticiones del silencio trabajan las diferencias de lo mismo. La luz combate la oscuridad que lleva adentro.

A Jorge Boccanera

CLXXV

Voids of being are unearthed in the explorations of the tongue. Why is it unable to name the fruits of hate after hate, potential roses, the questions a child may pose to his corner? Avanti, beast that seeks the body's lucid parts. What on earth does it all have to do with its arabesques, the alphabet of its mud, the rubble of its courage. That danger is a letter composed of initial vowels, disorders of the Z, a solitary bone in the jungle of explanations / inscriptions that fix the pinnacle of radiance.

For Alejandro García Schnetzer

CLXXV

La lengua que se explora encuentra los vacíos de ser. ¿Por qué no puede nombrar frutos del odio tras el odio, rosas posibles, las interrogaciones del niño a su rincón? Avanti, bestia que busca las partes lúcidas del cuerpo. Qué tiene que ver con sus decoraciones, el alfabeto de su barro, los despojos de su valentía. Ese peligro es una carta de iniciales vocálicas, trastornos de la zeta, el hueso solo en la selva de las explicaciones / marcas que atan el techo del fulgor.

A Alejandro García Schnetzer

CLXXVI

The phonetics of logic do not own its heart. The lacunae vanish in the and-yets of the reflection that eats its own innards. The fair damsel avenged her malaise and there is so much world groveling below. Sentences are bastardly tunnels without a single gesture of invention and their discourse has neither a dash nor a gash from the rueful soul. Things that exist on account of their not existing greet Pythagoras and tradition weeps. The upmost third of the sky surmises the repetition, making gestures no one cares to comprehend.

CLXXVI

Las fonéticas de la lógica no son dueñas de su corazón. Las lagunas se van en todavías del reflejo que come sus entrañas. La doncella muy fermosa vengó su padecer y hay tanto mundo que se humilla. Las sentencias son túneles bastardos sin gestos de invención y su discurso no tiene rayos ni rajas del alma pobrecita. Las cosas que son porque no son saludan a Pitágoras y la costumbre llora. El tercio superior del cielo vislumbra la repetición y hace gestos que nadie quiere entender.

CLXXVII

Science, a science sadder than science. The city doctor doesn't probe his symptoms / hollow echo in the stomach / murmurs in the smoky lungs / fires of the gall bladder / the heart in contradiction with all the numbers. Mallarme's sole star died as if it were still the object of desire. Diamond winks, clientless effigies, *s'i' fosse fuoco*, a blind Cecco, who, dispossessed, descended to the depths of the sea. The struggles of Eros hush beneath the forests of air that will deform them.

CLXXVII

Ciencia, ciencia más triste que la ciencia. El médico de la ciudad no investiga sus síntomas / el ruido a vacío de su estómago / los murmullos de su pulmón ahumado / fuegos de la vesícula / el corazón a contramano de las numeraciones. La única estrella de Mallarmé murió como si la quisiera todavía. Son los mohines del diamante, efigies sin cliente, *s'i' fosse fuoco*, Cecco ciego que bajó a mares sin amparo. Las luchas de Eros callan bajo los bosques de aire que las deformarán.

CLXXVIII

The poem's hapax needs no documentation, born because it was born to counter the poverty of the tongue / a magnolia dying of drought. The sideslip of the pensicula olivensis unsettles those eyes determined to see only what they see. Energy broils in the underbelly of the verses, strange voices the lifedeath dictionary fails to gloss. Raise your arms, you words that seize the not-said in your said! For you a voiceless law has fashioned invisible beasts.

CLXXVIII

El hápax de un poema no necesita documentos. Nació porque nació contra pobrezas de la lengua / una magnolia se murió sin agua. Los derrapes de la pensícula olivensis desarreglan los ojos empeñados en ver sólo lo que ven. En la interioridad de los versículos bullen energías, voces extrañas que el diccionario de la vidamuerte nunca anota. ¡Alcen los brazos, palabras que atrapan el no decir de su decir! Una ley muda les construyó animales invisibles.

CLXXIX

Who gathers round the pendulum / what human malice / comes goes with sluggish blades? Exquisite fables? The future laden with what was not? Starless hands live on a loose leaf / things that remain / accidents of perfection. Do they lie in the word mañana / balsam on the edge of blood / does it / bring new silences / the unearther / mañana / untouched?

CLXXIX

¿Quién se reúne alrededor del péndulo / qué miserias humanas / vienen van con los cuchillos lentos? ¿Fábulas exquisitas / el porvenir cargado de lo que no fue? En una hoja viven manos sin astros / cosas que quedan / accidentes de la perfección. ¿Están en la palabra mañana / bálsamo al borde de la sangre / trae silencios nuevos / ella / la desocultadora / ella / la no tocada?

CLXXX

The poem I wish to write for you, amouramour, has not yet a word. It travels in its negations and disasters like the yesterday in today and its plot is a flame. No one can extinguish it, guarding its secret when your face fills with wonder, opening doors for the subject, sacrifices of the when, two circles with no original composer.

CLXXX

El poema que te quiero escribir, amoramor, no tiene palabra todavía. Viaja en sus negaciones y desastres como el ayer en hoy y su argumento es una llama. Nadie puede apagarla y guarda su secreto cuando tu rostro es plena maravilla. Abre todas las puertas del sujeto, sacrificios del cuándo, los círculos de dos sin redactor original.

CLXXXI

The sign speaks of what does not exist / no interpreter, no moral piety. Other senses question it, the being's fable, the actual movement suppressing it. The end's revision draws near the face of the love that touches neither water nor soil, and grace is / no debt. Passion queries every mouth and onto its residue fall drops of failure. The no-man's forest gives lessons on inclemency / the worthy war of hopes / its infamy / heat with no fire.

CLXXXI

El signo habla de lo que no existe / sin intérprete ni piedad moral. Otros sentidos lo interrogan, la fábula de ser, el movimiento real que lo suprime. La revisión del fin acerca el rostro del amor que no pisa agua ni tierra y gracia es / no deuda. La pasión pregunta a cada boca y en sus residuos caen las gotas del fracaso. El bosque de ninguno da clases de mal tiempo / la buena guerra de las esperanzas / sus infamias / una calor sin fuego.

CLXXXII

Fear has a crazy patient. He's apt to traverse unlikelihoods to reach the moment that cannot be touched. Warblings, lings, things.

CLXXXII

El espanto tiene un enfermo loco. Es capaz de cruzar imposibles para ir al momento que no se puede tocar. Gorjeos, jeos eso.

CLXXXIII

Once upon a place in time aesthetics enjoyed not a single successful gala. Splendid / catastrophe of our epoch / she weeps a bit / imposing beheadings of life. Exogenous perception of the subjective sludge makes her just another number / a package / a tatter of the system. The moribund hoist the folds of the instant. Fish become pure scales in the simple unity of tranquil seas. Under the moon endure the natural fires of chains and populations of the verge of destruction. Eyes that penetrate the lunacy of lamps / solid love / warbling forests / sentiments of sense / losses of cultivated reason.

CLXXXIII

Estábase la estética en un lugar sin galas exitosas. La espléndida / desastre de este tiempo / poco llora / impone degollaciones de la vida. La percepción exógena del fango subjetivo la convierte en un número más / un paquete / un trapo del sistema. Los moribundos alzan los pliegues del instante. El pecho escama peces en la simple unidad de mares quietos. Debajo de la luna habita el fuego natural de las cadenas y poblados vecinos de la destrucción. Ojos que entran en la locura de las lámparas / el firme amor / los bosques que gorjean / los sentimientos del sentido / derrotas de la culta razón.

CLXXXIV

Love / moves toward desire without fear of destiny. Illuminated by hypotheses, a chance warbler, a bridge that excludes itself, it bears the burden of its wounds / nighttime, its pay / the annulment of all light / the glaucous copper of old passion. The rose awaits rising up beneath the knives of the moon. No one will overpower its cherubim or steal its casque / the valiant adventure. Reason that violates illusion has no virgins / rhythms of joy / it falls like a pauper / bereft of doors / of pardon.

CLXXXIV

Amor / va al deseo y no teme al destino. Lo iluminan hipótesis, un pájaro casual, el puente que se excluye. Carga con sus heridas / su salario es la noche / la anulación de toda luz / el cobre verde de la vieja pasión. La rosa espera vertical bajo cuchillos de la luna. Nadie se apoderará de sus querubes ni le quitarán el casco / la aventura valiente. La razón que violenta a la ilusión no tiene vírgenes / ritmos de la dicha / cae pobre / sin puerta / sin perdón.

CLXXXV

The flesh, the bone, the liver's warnings, answers never there, nor hints of a cause. Closures of the concept drift in images of its withered beauty. Drinkers, fornicators, making an oasis of the desert where a woman on fire is heard in song. It is one of desire's sojourns where the mutations are deep. Hermeneutics can fathom nothing and the body's dusks become muddled with the country that is always leaving. The victims are oblivious of their victim's first tongue.

CLXXXV

La carne, el hueso, advertencias del hígado, respuestas que no hay, ni sombras de un origen. Clausuras del concepto vagan en las imágenes de su belleza ajada. Los bebedores, los fornicadores, crean oasis del desierto donde se escuchan músicas de una mujer que arde. Es un paraje del deseo donde las mutaciones son más hondas. La hermenéutica no entiende nada y se mezclan las tinieblas del cuerpo con un país que cada vez se va. Las víctimas ignoran el lenguaje primero de su víctima.

CLXXXVI

When reason turns tender, autumn will cease to shed its leaves. They will become conundrums of being / yellow / useless / blind to their mother's face / delusions of things. They need to see, taste, hear, touch a dog, listen to their passion, leave the ruins of writing behind. The will's tension dances in the square meters of time. In such a fashion there once bloomed a flower the centuries cannot touch / love sweats.

For Víctor Sandoval
In memoriam

CLXXXVI

Cuando la razón sea sensible el otoño no tirará sus hojas. Serán incógnitas del ser / amarillas / inútiles / no verán el rostro de su madre / las alucinaciones de las cosas. Necesitan oído, gusto, ver, tocar un perro, escuchar su pasión, dejar atrás ruinas de la escritura. En los metros cuadrados del tiempo danzan tensiones de la voluntad. Así nació una flor que los siglos no pueden tocar / el amor suda.

A Víctor Sandoval
In memoriam

CLXXXVII

You leave the writing to greet the world and the world sends you back to the writing. The heart, the liver, the mother's medulla have no other way to live. Let the savages come touch this maze / they will find themselves trounced in the transformation of the invisible. Fingers touching the untouchable bask like a child in his crib. No need for them to beg their bread. They soar in probity and so come to know their own infernos.

For Antonio Gamoneda

CLXXXVII

Salís de la escritura al mundo y el mundo te vuelve a la escritura. El corazón, el hígado, la entraña de la madre, no tienen otra manera de vivir. Que vengan los salvajes a tocar este dédalo y serán derrotados en la transformación de lo invisible. Dedos que tocan lo intocable se recrean como niño en su cuna. No necesitan mendigar su pan. Vuelan en la bondad y así conocen sus infiernos.

A Antonio Gamoneda

CLXXXVIII

Ovid invented *fin'amor* and no one paid him heed. He sought sounds with words and love, which scorn goads into caves / his skin grows lined with wrinkles / face dry as dust. Not in sorrowful knights, shepherdesses of fresh bodies and feelings chaste, repose in leafy shade. The accidents of transmission lessen the delight / the tail-thrashing of a world set free. In nocturnal beds the quest for the human alphabet bleeds / the invention of shadowless passions.

CLXXXVIII

Ovidio inventó el *fins amor* y no le hicieron caso. Buscó sonidos con palabras y el amor que el rechazo manda a cuevas / se le arruga la piel / el rostro se evapora. No en caballeros tristes, las pastoras de cuerpo nuevo y casto sentimiento, descansos en la umbría. Los accidentes de la transmisión achican el deleite / coletazos del mundo en libertad. En los lechos nocturnos se desangra la búsqueda del alfabeto humano / la invención de pasiones sin sombras.

CLXXXIX

An uncertain madness turns blood into fire and blazes against the words where centuries accrue. The brightly-colored past creaks and no one knows where the one who left wound up, love sullied by a difficult light. Fury mounts the blind under a frosty moon, and fathers, mothers, children lay a silence of flowers on the pleas of the departed. The A of my nightingale could switch to your B-flat, which would change what? Yours / theirs / whose / plunder vulnerable albums / anger skies of azure coal.

CLXXXIX

Una locura incierta cambia la sangre en fuego y arde contra palabras en las que se amontonan siglos. Chirría el pasado de color vivísimo y no se sabe dónde quedó el que fue, el amor maculado por una luz difícil. La furia monta ciegos bajo la luna helada y padres, madres, hijos depositan un silencio de flores sobre las súplicas del ido. Se puede convertir en sí el mí del ruiseñor, eso qué arregla. El tuyo / el suyo / el cuyo vacían álbumes inermes / enojan cielos de carbón azul.

CXC

In the sea one hears when a tree hides its shame for crimes
against it / the other / you / the unruly word expels destiny's
quasi shriek. Each day emerges and its untenable height
explains that to explain the absence is another absence.
A damsel veils the page of a tale, the counted days of the
sun's right to set. To walk the earth is to tremble in the
contradictions of the love for you and my love for you,
world assailed by celestial iciness. It strikes the upright word
in its hale or rain that soaks the invisible.

For Alberto Díaz

CXC

En el mar que se oye cuando un árbol esconde su vergüenza
por crímenes contra él / el otro / vos / la palabra rebelde
expulsa al casi llanto de la fatalidad. Se asoma cada día y su
altura insostenible explica que explicar la ausencia es otra
ausencia. Una doncella cubre la página del cuento, los días
contados del derecho a poner el sol en sí. Pisar la tierra es
temblar en las contradicciones del amor por vos y mi amor
por vos, mundo atacado por frialdades celestes. Golpean la
palabra erguida en su granizo o lluvia que moja lo invisible.

A Alberto Díaz

CXCI

Stone for a bed, the pillage of dreams slumbers, bit by bit the tongue jumps from memory to the price of a flower by ploughing it under. You can smell what occurred with each rising sun, from here departing, remaining here. The executed show their holes gorged with patience, moving in bottles still crossing seas. Glimmers of the zero offer up what they do not know in those failed interruptions. New ignominy is born, which night conceals with obligations. Stars on high.

For Marco Antonio Campos

CXCI

En una piedra duerme el saqueo del sueño, la lengua a pedacitos salta de la memoria al precio de una flor surcándola. Se respira lo que pasó en cada día que llega, irse de aquí, quedarse aquí. Los fusilados muestran sus aujeros ahítos de paciencia, se van en las botellas que cruzan mares todavía. Brillos del cero dan lo que no saben en los fracasos de la interrupción. Nacen infamias nuevas que la noche oculta con obligaciones. Astros encima.

A Marco Antonio Campos

CXCII

Silence escapes through the window / maintaining processional fixities / harmonies that will not be / with morning they have done what? The tears that drench the blind man's halves disappear without waves. What became of the violent light where touching whatever can't be seen? Hand with neither music nor autumn to turn it into favors for May. The alternative days of the outside are studied by the love that sups.

For José Ángel Leyva

CXCII

El silencio huye por la ventana / guarda fijezas del cortejo / armonías que no serán / de la mañana han hecho qué. Las lágrimas que mojan las mitades del ciego desaparecen sin oleaje. ¿Dónde quedó la luz violenta donde tocar qué no se ve? Mano sin música ni otoño que la convierta en favores de mayo. Los días alternos del afuera son revisados por el amor que come.

A José Ángel Leyva

CXCIII

Whisper to the word to see what it says against the discourse
of unhappiness. Will anyone pay it heed on the roads
that succeed the father? Is to move against the subject the
beginning of wisdom? On the edges of the spectacle, feces
of hope. The patches of the long-since lead to bolting fevers
/ invitations to forget pages torn in two.

For Jorge Boccanera

CXCIII

Háblenle al oído a la palabra ver qué dice contra el discurso
de la infelicidad. ¿Se le hará caso en los caminos que
suceden al padre? ¿Andar contra el sujeto es el comienzo de
la sabiduría? Al borde del espectáculo, heces de la esperanza.
Los parches del mucho tiempo derivan en fiebres galopantes
/ invitaciones a olvidar papeles rotos.

A Jorge Boccanera

CXCIV

The skylark didn't want them to dirty her / she said the end / the end. The end she said / not wanting them to dirty her / the end. Bred to write her gift of flight / the end. Dripping wet when she said the end in the alleys of dark wisdom / strokes of madness. It had been a blow, and she said the end / they're killing everything around us / the end. She cracked the locks of evil / flashes of the furious heart / the end. The skylark said the end.

CXCIV

La alondra no quiso que la ensucien / dijo fin / dijo fin. Dijo fin / no quiso que la ensucien / dijo fin. Criada para escribir su dádiva de vuelo / dijo fin. Goteaba cuando dijo fin en callejones del saber oscuro / trazos de la locura. Era sorpresa y dijo fin / matan todo alrededor / dijo fin. Abrió cerrojos de la maldad / resplandores del corazón furioso / dijo fin. La alondra dijo fin.

CXCV

Huapangos in the Coahuila desert, just listen. The clatter of dancing bones resounds beyond the museum, it says life, it's what was there before the breeze picked up. There they remain, eternity does not visit them, there are only lead seals on censored writs or a muteness that covers tragedies / the remembrance of struggles long gone is not what keeps them going. The lots cast are fixed in motionless breaths / mirrors of no return.

For Alberto Szpunberg

CXCV

En el desierto de Coahuila hay huapangos, basta oír. El repique de los huesos resuena afuera del museo, dice vida, es lo que fue a la hora de la brisa. Ahí se quedan, la eternidad no los visita, sólo hay plomadas del atajo o una mudez que cubre las tragedias / no trabajan por recordar luchas idas. La suerte que se echó está fija en alientos inmóviles / espejos sin retorno.

A Alberto Szpunberg

CXCVI

Sorrow that finds no expression is cleft into a pair of trees that fall silent. The longing to crush the patient does not stem from enemy spittle. Who casts the dice for the meeting with the provisional song? The disguise trips on its own clothes and the plenary interpretation has lost its livid niches. The tongue pounds and pounds, saying what? Alcaeus *face down on the girl* in her beauty drinks without waiting till 8 p.m., the rudder snags on the father's cowardice. No other way to navigate the rivers where monkeys scream and splendor summons mutinous gold.

CXCVI

El dolor que no encuentra expresión se divide en dos árboles que callan. Las ganas de aplastar al paciente no viene de salivas enemigas. ¿Quién echa los dados del encuentro con la canción provisional? El disfraz tropieza con su ropa y la interpretación plenaria perdió sus lívidos rincones. El machaque y machaque de la lengua ¿dice algo? Alceo *cara abajo en la muchacha* linda bebe sin esperar las 8 de la noche, se le enreda el timón en cobardías del padre. No se navega de otro modo en ríos donde los monos gritan y el esplendor convoca oros amotinados.

CXCVII

Swaps at the level of perception shake up the soul / thrushes
reserve their warbles. Where is the how that is never taught?
In the foothills shreds of nature settle, horses disappear in
a single night / screams and clubbings cannot restore their
canter. In what space can speech turn into place? Beyond the
tongue there are corpses of artificiality / an oven incinerates
machines of the breaking point.

CXCVII

Los trueques del nivel perceptivo zarandean el ánima /
zorzales ahorran su gorjeo. ¿A dónde va el cómo que no
puede enseñar? Al pie de la montaña caen desgarros de la
naturaleza, caballos desaparecen en una sola noche / gritos y
bastonazos no recuperan su galope. ¿En qué espacio el decir
se convierte en lugar? Hay fuera de la lengua cadáveres de
la artificialidad / un horno quema las máquinas del límite.

CXCVIII

Poetry feeds on life / as is logical. How else can the lungs breathe, or the egret I never saw, the faceless message? Representation noiselessly dies in the lion's jaws. One must gaze into the interior jungle though evil slither from its box. Time is never distracted from the misery afflicting its goblet / it flings metric manuals / theories on death / making love far and wide. Autumn's private life has leaves that never fall.

CXCVIII

La poesía come vida / con razón. ¿De qué otro modo respiran los pulmones, la garza que no vi, el mensaje sin rostro? La representación muere sin ruido en los mordiscos del león. Hay que mirarse la selva adentro aunque el mal salga de su caja. El tiempo nunca se distrae de las penas que afligieron su copa / tira manuales de la métrica / teorías de la muerte / hace el amor en cualquier parte. La vida privada del otoño tiene hojas que no caen.

CXCIX

The high altar where one ruminates the body possesses unruly virtuosities. What does one do with blind passions? They may die in public applause / sprigs of sage / the one, nonexistent. The system's beasts will decide upon their tongue, what to do with its glow. A tree blocks the breasts of the young with the shade of what one day they will proffer.

For Andrea

CXCIX

El altar mayor donde se rumia el cuerpo tiene virtuosidades sin control. ¿Qué hacer con sus pasiones ciegas? Pueden morir en aplausos del público, ramas de salvia, el uno que no existe. Las bestias del sistema decidirán su lengua, qué hacer con su fulgor. Un árbol tapa el pecho de los jóvenes con la sombra de lo que van a dar.

A Andrea

CC

Intensity, duration, the number of fallen syllables affect both the good and the wicked. What remains hidden is reserved for night. On impossible mornings men pass by. No one regards the language of the found, its formulas broken so they won't be read. Farewell said the hunger, the orange, the slave's internal work, rhythms beyond the tongue.

CC

La intensidad, la duración, el número de sílabas caídas tocan a buenos y a malvados. Lo oculto es para la noche. Pasan hombres de mañana imposible. Nadie mira el lenguaje del hallado, sus fórmulas rompidas para que no se lean. Adiós decían el hambre, la naranja, los trabajos internos del esclavo, el ritmo fuera de la lengua.

CCI

Tyrannies of goodness / convocation of the storm / shudders of the almost. The torch that burns in the returned / blood that reached the opal. Such excess of heart in those who spoke, their child would open notebooks, the walls of a single syllable, the laws of grace. The body's circulation through lies of what is real / misfortunes of the we / hunger that can be heard here below. The tongue utters gunshots for those engrossed in fables of the gold.

CCI

Tiranías de la bondad / convocación de la tormenta / los tiembles del apenas. La antorcha que arde en el volvido / sangre que llegó al ópalo. Y cuánto corazón demás en los que hablaron, su niño abría cuadernos, los muros de una sílaba, las leyes de la gracia. Circulación del cuerpo por falsedades del real / desgracias del nosotros / hambres que se oyen acá abajo. La lengua dice tiros al ocupado en fábulas del oro.

CCII

Thought falls into lengthy measures of the matter / sitting in robberies of life / the remains of the vestibule / neither by you for me nor by me for you. Pleasure finds no delight in changing / discussing deceits in its amorphous potential. Childhood spins in gyres / the rites of the uncreated mouth. The I know has spies that no longer toil.

CCII

El pensamiento cae en largas del asunto / se sienta en robos de la vida / los restos del vestíbulo / ni a mí por vos ni a vos por mí. El goce no quiere cambiar / discurre engaños en su potencia amorfa. La infancia gira en espiral / los ritos de la boca increada. El yo sé tiene espías que no trabajan más.

CCIII

In the substance of the source lie cities shrouded in jungle canopies and symptoms of collection. Layers of fog, one atop the other, protect the gold's can-can dance, fashionable to sign contracts with blindness, silence, a clothespinned nose, oblivious to hunger on the street. From which ego or other might they have fallen? Wretchedness does not pick them up and the dankness of the escapes drenches them to the bone. Pieces of humiliation, stumps, bruises from the tomb. Strange roses are born in chemical hells and the image dies in the lacuna. Tangents of the tongue continue working in order to ward off sleep.

CCIII

En las sustancias del origen hay ciudades cubiertas por la selva y síntomas de colección. Capas de la neblina, una a una, protegen el can-can del oro, es moda firmar contratos con la ceguera, la mudez, el tapadón de la nariz, no ver hambre en la calle. ¿De qué algún yo cayeron? No los recoge la miseria y la humedad de los fugados les moja hasta los huesos. Pedazos de la humillación, muñones, machacas de la bóveda. Extrañas rosas nacen de los infiernos químicos y la imagen se muere en la laguna. Tangentes de la lengua trabajan para no dormir.

CCIV

The ruins of nations survive in the pauses of deceit. The magnificence of the national flag, pledges that decompose the creature's edges, its warren. A complement locks itself inside a girl immersed in the abstraction. Scraps of love wet the black, unfathomable rock, the bitter sobbing of their confession. Hup, hup, warm hearts, the defeat is ours, galloping unprotected on the Pampas.

CCIV

Las ruinas de los pueblos sobreviven en las paradas del engaño. Magnificencias del escudo nacional, el juramento que deshace filos de la criatura, su guarida. Un complemento se encierra en una niña tendida en la abstracción. Restos de amor mojan la roca negra incomprensible, la confesión con amarguras que lloraban. Arriba, corazones, que la derrota es nuestra, galopa en pampas sin cobijo.

CCV

Springtime avoids the succession of double stresses. They take shelter under the sun of hardships sung, the rules of short syllables, running off to freedom's bogs. And who has glimpsed their faces? No one knows if they drink the sounds of the seas from Sappho or from the serpent of Stesichorus. Or from yet some other vein.

CCV

La primavera evita la sucesión de dos acentos. Se amparan bajo el sol de desdichas cantadas, las reglas de la sílaba corta, se van a los pantanos de la libertad. ¿Y quién les vio la cara alguna vez? Nadie sabe si beben el sonido de los mares en Safo o en la serpiente de Estesícoro. O en otras venas todavía.

CCVI

Healing / worsening the wound they return with their questions. Yesteryear's fire pays no compensation for the consequences. Are these, are those the pieces I was? The body / there are no banquets / the narrowing of the stage cannot shut enormously wakeful eyes. That blood over there, the intermediate product of wishes. The dream I dream / dream / I dream. In one single night.

For Lucila Pagliai

CCVI

Curar / empeorar la herida vuelven con sus preguntas. El ardor del antaño no paga consecuencias. ¿Son éstos, son aquéllos, los pedazos del fui? El cuerpo / no hay banquetes / la reducción del escenario no cierra ojazos muy despiertos. Sangres aquéllas, el producto intermedio de las ganas. El sueño sueño / sueño / sueño. En una sola noche.

A Lucila Pagliai

CCVII

Hard-times brothers soon recognize each other. We swim and find a name without meaning, parodies of the rhythmic accent, transactions with the final distance. Sweat soaks the patient / the burning of a park where he fell into a woman. The embryo of a look is happier than the look / calculations of being-here fail to soil it / not the being's bandoneon / not the backdropped curtain. Childhood assesses the sorrows of what occurred and thus lives in the part that was ravaged.

For Jorge Boccanera

CCVII

Los hermanos en la desdicha se reconocen pronto. Nadamos y encontramos nombre sin significación, parodias del acento rítmico, transacciones con la distancia última. El sudor moja al paciente / la quemazón del parque donde se hundió en una mujer. El embrión de una mirada es más feliz que la mirada / no lo ensucian los cálculos de estar / ni el bandoneón de ser / ni la cortina al fondo. La niñez averigua tristezas de lo que pasó y así vive en su parte embestida.

A Jorge Boccanera

CCVIII

Intimacies of the tongue never rest, they push and push to name a blade within the conscience, a bird at the nape, marble made of cardboard. Who if not they might realize, who if not they might recognize cities by the smoke of human misery? A woman plants herself on boulders tinged with their blood. In her secret coffer fury is a broken circle and common evil comes sauntering into her home.

For Cristina Banegas

CCVIII

Las entretelas de la lengua no descansan, pujan y pujan para nombrar un puñal en la conciencia, un pájaro en la nuca, mármoles de cartón. ¿Quién si no ellas saben, quién si no ellas conocen ciudades por el humo de la miseria humana? Una mujer se planta en piedras teñidas con su sangre. En su estuche secreto la furia es un círculo roto y entra en la casa el mal común.

A Cristina Banegas

CCIX

Wine grows sad in an empty glass. Squinting, the sun regards the untenanted chair / the events of its desolation / commanders of the absence / the mirroring tree that never forgets its task. The distance of a bird to its bird has neither name nor script. The night's second guest performs a famous feat / a rose without water / testimony from a nonexistent verse.

CCIX

El vino es triste en la copa vacía. Con párpados oblicuos el sol mira la silla sin nadie / los acontecimientos de su desolación / los jefes de la ausencia / árbol especular que nunca olvida su trabajo. Las distancias de un pájaro a su pájaro no tienen nombre ni escritura. El segundo invitado de la noche crea un hecho famoso / una rosa sin agua / testimonios del verso que no existe.

CCX

Love's distance has faces it knows not / now or ever. The gesture crumples in the sublimations of itself, airs where launch and finale resound. Within the body are communications that crackle / conspire with surprises / the rain / the earth / the ashes of compassion. Rhythms that mute their meanings / deconstruction of the bird / interminable deferment under heaven's vault / the unbearable damage.

CCX

La lejanía del amor tiene rostros que no conoce / no conocerá. El gesto se arruga en las sublimaciones de sí mismo, aires donde resuenan el comienzo y el corte. En el cuerpo hay comunicaciones que crepitan / pactan con las sorpresas / la lluvia / la tierra / cenizas de la compasión. Ritmos que callan su sentido / deconstrucción del pájaro / esperas bajo el cielo / el daño insoportable.

CCXI

Stupor crafts analogies of a longing shackled on beaches of dispassion. The appetite for what came before is satiated in vile conveyance / reconsiderations as regards one's hide. Fear gnaws at the dignity of the tetrameter / better to die standing than to live on one's knees. The darkness of being lies in locked rooms.

CCXI

El estupor ve identidades del deseo maniatado en playas de la despasión. El apetito de lo que pasó se sacia en transferencias viles / reconsideraciones del pellejo. El temor masca la dignidad del heptasílabo / mejor morir de pie que vivir de rodillas. Se encuentra la oscuridad de ser en un cuarto cerrado.

CCXII

The I's weeds block the word's light, bar its flight. Open to the blood's sky / the chest's skin is flayed in the singular instant / what is seen is not seen / naked steps. The battered part of the I brews impenetrable mists. Dazzling afternoons feed a dwindling of the great fatigue. Arrows shot toward centerless circles perform to empty halls.

CCXII

Las malezas del yo cierran la luz a la palabra, no la dejan salir. Al cielo abierto de la sangre / la piel del pecho despegada en el instante único / lo que se ve no se ve / pasos desnudos. El maltrato del yo crea neblinas y no se puede entrar. En los deslumbramientos de la tarde crece una reducción del gran cansancio. Flechas al círculo sin centro actúan en salones vacíos.

CCXIII

A song frozen stiff in realities wishes to return to its real /
always heading toward questions / pursuing presumptions.
The knife's froth moistens what it cuts / the excesses of one's
own end / its vacillating name. In the enunciation's mirror,
spineless tremors do not appear / the bone's doubts / the
domestication of the self's unease / the mutilating valor.
What's left behind is an arid country / unpeopled alleys /
actions even or odd / parables of the lost womb. Scorching.

For Ignacio Uranga

CCXIII

Un canto yerto en realidades quiere volver a su real / se
va siempre a preguntas / persigue presunciones. Espumas
del cuchillo mojan lo que corta / excesos del fin propio /
su nombre vacilante. En el espejo de la enunciación no
aparecen temblores de la cobardía / dudas del hueso / la
domesticación de la inquietud de sí / el valor que mutila.
Lo atrás dejado es un seco país / callejones sin ciudadanía /
actos pares o nones / parábolas del útero perdido. Quema.

A Ignacio Uranga

CCXIV

Brains without thirst don't bloom in the sun. With stolid medullae they conduct cross-sectional studies to calm their time, never glowing in rhabdomancies that search for footsteps in the abyss, rums of death, the black / white of the line. They have chiseled their discourse, and to them the era's disasters dictate vacuous pages.

CCXIV

Los cerebros sin sed no tienen carnaciones al sol. Hacen estudios transversales para tranquilizar su tiempo con médula apagada. No arden en rabdomancias que buscan pisadas del abismo, cachazas de la muerte, el negro / blanco de la línea. Pintaron su discurso y las desgracias de la época les dictan páginas en blanco.

CCXV

Worrisome to leave the night that falls from an absence. It brings love / that one time it said now / witnesses of whim. Why abandon its ship? The I stirs its exiles with silent hands / liquid thoughts from below / the smoke's ribcage. No wind to pacify the crickets / night held in their power.

CCXV

Preocupa dejar la noche que cae de una ausencia. Trae amor / la vez que dijo ahora / testigos del capricho. ¿Para qué irse de su barco? El yo revuelve sus exilios con las manos calladas / el pensamiento líquido de abajo / las costillas del humo. No hay viento que apacigüe a los grillos / tienen la noche en su poder.

CCXVI

Beneath the leafless bower the specter appears / arrayed in white / it slips behind the eye. A craving to gorge on it in daylight's food. No one knows its domains / soundless / tasteless. Bringing a wound exposed to the lack / into cruder species it drives its sword.

CCXVI

Bajo las enramadas secas entra la aparición / viste de blanco / se va detrás del ojo. Ansias de hartarse de ella en la comida de los días. Nadie conoce sus regiones / sin sonido / sin sabor. Trae una herida abierta a lo faltante / clava su espada en las especies crudas.

CCXVII

The shawl went down to the river *where love abounds* /
plants of departure began to grow / extinguishing the rose
and the solace of the rose / its shadow / sheltering corners of
the cradle / virgin skin / horses made of air that still remain.
Aromas of liquid thoughts touch blind ears. She who weeps
at the unalterable cross bears broken kisses / wins battles
she lost.

For Chavela Vargas
In memoriam
Mexico City, August 5, 2012

CCXVII

El rebozo fue al río *donde se quiere más* / crecieron plantas
de irse. Apagaron la rosa y su consuelo / la sombra de la rosa
/ cubre rincones de la cuna / pieles vírgenes / caballos de
aire que se quedan. Aromas del pensamiento líquido tocan
oídos ciegos. La que llora de cruz inalterable carga con besos
rotos / gana batallas que perdió.

A Chavela Vargas
In memoriam
Ciudad de México, 5 de agosto 2012

CCXVIII

The ephemeral lingers in alleyways where love exists and things come crashing down / the moment that was / the one that will be. The matter that leaves footprints cannot be weighed / measured / the fleetingness of its kin. Where is it heading, where did the smithless brand come from? Could it be the stamp that mistrusts language? Neither being / nor eternity / nor essence in what is real, which tolerates everything. Not even a child who remembers his old age.

For Ignacio Uranga

CCXVIII

Lo efímero dura en callejones donde amor hay y todo se derrumba / la vez que fue / la que será. La materia que deja huellas no se puede pesar / medir / fugacidad de sus parientes. ¿A dónde va, de dónde viene la marca sin herrero? ¿Será la impronta que desconfía del lenguaje? Ni ser / ni eternidad / ni esencia en el real que todo aguanta. Ni un niño que recuerde su vejez.

A Ignacio Uranga

CCXIX

He pulls back the covers / the Boston Symphony unheard / the street's misery smashing the B-flats / the figure unfolding in order to be here now. The NASDAQ rises and falls in reserves of unpunished greed / John Donne invites *a woman of many men to share his bones on the final day* / William Count of Poitiers announces a poetry *about nothing at all.* What does the word say about once? To fall asleep atop a horse is to test representation / neither I / nor you / no one / nothing / *non sai.* Diseased, the name grows / cloisters itself from worldwide madness.

CCXIX

Abre la cama / no escucha la sinfónica de Boston / miserias en la calle desploman los bemoles / se abre la figura para estar. El Nasdaq sube y baja en reservorios de la codicia impune / John Donne invita a una *mujer de muchos hombres a compartir sus huesos el día final* / el Guillermo Poiters anuncia una poesía *sobre absolutamente nada.* ¿Qué dice la palabra de la vez? Dormir sobre un caballo reta a la representación / ni yo / ni vos / nadie / nada / *no sai.* El nombre crece enfermo / se enclaustra contra la locura mundial.

CCXX

In the gadgets of presage, a gaunt reason asks for a breather. It needs Michelangelo's *bellezza e grazia equalmente infinita*, his fête and pearls on behalf of human labor. The guest of the region's mien faces off with oblivion / an elixir overwhelms the wall. Seminars on naming are clueless as to the oaks of Chillán / the park / Chile.

CCXX

La razón flaca pide descanso en los dispositivos del presagio. Necesita la *bellezza e grazia equalmente infinita* de Miguel, su fiesta y perlas del trabajo humano. El huésped de los rostros de allá carea al olvido / un elixir sumerge al muro. Los seminarios de la designación no saben dónde están los robles de Chillán / plaza / Chile.

CCXXI

Speak? Fleeting elements appear / disappear with a fate unknown. Are we made / unmade? Do they unbind trees / were they not watered? Rationale exists for murdering the dead / incandescence / to rouse creatures / sluggish eroticism / the will of chaos. Splendor remains in a mortal's divisions / half toward horror / half toward self. Time finds him a roofless dwelling / silhouettes enter / poses of the word beautiful do not conceal its void.

CCXXI

¿Hablar? Elementos fugaces aparecen / desaparecen con destino ignorado. ¿Nos hacen / nos deshacen? ¿Desatan árboles / nadie los regó? Hay materia para matar a muertos / fulgores / despiertan criaturas / erotismos lentos / la voluntad del caos. Hay esplendor en divisiones del mortal / mitad hacia el horror / mitad hacia sí mismo. El tiempo le procura una casa sin techo / entran siluetas / las poses de la palabra bello no ocultan su vacío.

CCXXII

Love that soars in the belly of the word without circle or center / raises his arms at the silence of sons and fathers / nighttime instincts / origins / it's him. Textures of desire one longs to touch / energies without coffers / it's him / him. Flesh of another material / neither chair / nor coach / beyond all economy / it's him. With no advantages / with foldings and unfoldings / the blind unlock their sight / it's him.

CCXXII

Amor que vuela en el envés de una palabra sin círculo ni centro. Alza los brazos en silencios de hijos y padres / instintos de la noche / orígenes / es él. Texturas del deseo que se quieren tocar / energías sin cofre / es él / es él. Carne de otra materia / ni silla / ni vagón / fuera de toda economía / es él. Sin ventajas / con pliegues y despliegues / el ciego abre la vista / es él.

CCXXIII

Sleeping beauties apportion guilt, measure the time of the flesh. Fury lost its music and searches for union with itself in any falling pitch / things paired up by passion sign no documents. Leo the Hebrew would laugh at the technical measurements of a body like one who laughs lugging tiny bones / rolling / banging against the bier / they will speak with the soil. Love whistles at one side or other of disaster, no one kneads the flour of the moon. In the shreds of history free kisses endure / wandering beauties that keep evil at bay / in new seasons you were heard in song so that everyone might find union / o banished soul!

For Luis Chumacero

CCXXIII

Las bellas durmientes reparten culpas, miden los tiempos de la carne. La furia perdió música y busca unión consigo misma en cualquier dejo despeñado / lo que une la pasión no firma documentos. León Hebreo se reía de las medidas técnicas de un cuerpo / como el que ríe con huesitos al hombro / ruedan / golpean el cajón / hablarán con la tierra. El amor silba a un lado y otro del desastre, nadie amasa la harina de la luna. En los andrajos de la historia quedaron besos libres / hermosuras errantes para que el mal se abaje / en estaciones nuevas te oyeron cantar para que todos se unan / oh expulsado.

A Luis Chumacero

CCXXIV

The sun of Rome gilded new ineptitudes and morphine for lacerations of the spirit does not exist. They gather their impossibilities and thus learn to live / creating memories of what was ignored / useless to seek them out. My father, in a photograph, cane hooked on his left arm / so distant the kerchief covering his hammer / the saw / the nails of his craft in a silence without a country. Are there faces missing from what we were in the calendars of plunder? Blake said to the sickly rose, *O Rose, thou art sick*, said William Blake.

CCXXIV

El sol de Roma doró impotencias nuevas y no hay morfina para laceraciones del espíritu. Juntan sus imposibles y así aprenden a vivir / crean memorias de lo ignorado / inútil las buscar. Mi padre en una foto, bastón en brazo izquierdo / tan lejos el pañuelo que cubre su martillo / la sierra / los clavos del oficio en un silencio sin república. ¿Faltan rostros que fuimos en calendarios del despojo? Blake le dijo a la rosa que está enferma, *estás enferma, rosa*, le dijo William Blake.

CCXXV

The Reaper keeps his nose to the grindstone / pointless to invoke him / opening chests / taking pictures / which is which. Time yellows I remember / the navigating grapheme always missing / so many graces lost. He who organizes his own shipwreck cannot hear the crepitation of the wait. Intimate oblivion lurks to see if the little girl was alive / if the mother was alive / birth in a police car / she shines in the great palace of her mother. Humankind looks like a dictionary with words in tenements of the abyss.

CCXXV

La Huesuda se limita a trabajar / inútil que la invoquen / abre un cajón / saca fotos / cuál de ellos será quién. El tiempo amarilla a lo recuerdo / siempre falta la letra que navega / gracias tantas perdidas. El que organiza su naufragio no oye crepitaciones de la espera. Los olvidos cercanos acechan si la niña vivía y la madre vivía. La parida en un coche policial brilla en el gran palacio de su madre. Gente parece un diccionario con palabras en los inquilinatos del vacío.

CCXXVI

Where now is the desert with waters from my self? The ink of pain's reeditions pales. Wine, wind, tides bottled up in dissonant riches / artistry / the return of the old samovar / tea surrounded by its own perfection. Within the mantled child lie compassions of the absence / golden embers / disasters of the mother and the father / longings to snuggle in love to discover their pacts / bodies that reproduce him in free innocence. Hiking up their hills / sinister lyres in sight.

CCXXVI

¿Dónde quedó el desierto con aguas de mí mismo? Las reediciones del dolor pierden tinta. El vino, el viento, la marea enfrascados en riquezas inarmónicas / buenas artes / retornos del viejo samovar / el té rodeado de su perfección. En el niño que se tapó hay compasiones de la falta / ascuas de oro / desastres del padre y de la madre. Quiere meterse en el amor para saber sus pactos / cuerpos que reproducen al de enfrente en la inocencia libre. Trepar sus montes / liras siniestras a la vista.

CCXXVII

In breathing she is here / without praising herself / without knowing herself / without loving herself / her transcendence forbids it. Versions of her being-here trigger flights of prediction. Burning in her cheeks are trips the moon won't take / what is unfulfilled blindfolds the confinements her most secret eye breaks through. Her *fermosura vence a honestidade / tal amor, tanta fe, tanta verdade*. A song she sings without her / within her secret it conceals more soul than a finch in a chasmal flight.

CCXXVII

En la respiración ella está / sin alabarse / sin conocerse / sin amarse / su trascendencia lo prohíbe. Versiones de su estar causan el vuelo de la predicción. En su mejilla arden viajes que la luna no hará / lo incumplido venda encierros que su ojo más secreto rompe. Su *fermosura vence a honestidade / tal amor, tanta fe, tanta verdade*. Canta una canción sin ella / guarda en su secreto más del alma que jilguero en un vuelo abisal.

CCXXVIII

What is this matter without matter that suddenly falls like a lightning bolt? Who beckoned it, what is it made of, why does it not have whens or whys? Old man Plotinus / the one / the *nous* / he clothed orphans to find out. And on power's paths what could fatherless evils impart to you? The brand of the nonexistent iron, its mark with neither length nor weight nor fear of scars / or / wordless substances. Your ignorance / ours / is not consuming you / you involved in pristine fires.

CCXXVIII

¿Qué es esa materia sin materia que cae de pronto como rayo? ¿Quién la mandó llamar, de qué está hecha, por qué no tiene cuándos ni porqués? Viejo Plotino / el uno / el *nous* / abrigó huérfanos para saber. ¿Y qué podrían decirte males sin padre en los caminos de la fuerza? La impronta del hierro que no es, su marca sin longitud ni peso ni temor a cicatrices / o / sustancias sin palabra. No te consume tu ignorancia / nuestra / vos en fuegos limpios.

CCXXIX

Poem of harsh lineage / forefathers of the error / they will pronounce sentence when the proper one arrives. What will it do with such a dispersion of love, the word pursued in one's own jungles, that which is mined for gold? The breeze thickens the leaves / desolations tread on unsheltered words / burning stones. In every love, dearth is due to its hopelessness.

CCXXIX

Un poema con ascendencias duras / antepasados de la equivocación / dictarán su condena cuando la debida llegue. ¿Qué hará con tanto amor disperso, la palabra buscada en selvas de uno mismo, lo que se cava en busca de oro? La brisa espesa hojas / desolaciones pisan palabras sin cobijo / piedras que ardieron. En todo amor la falta es mérito de su imposible.

CCXXX

Where are you, Angel of Michel? *In foco ardente / e l'alma
perder se null'altro sente?* The truth of your arm transforms
the divine. To emerge from the self with a stone to offset
silenced love, that which is never finished so there may be
perfection in the loss. Dried bones *di Dio formatti /* eyes
entombed before their time. It is the spirit of the fruition of
love deprived / the superior portion of the inferior leaves it
all on his tendered platter.

CCXXX

¿Dónde estás, Angel de Miguel? *¿In foco ardente / e l'alma
perder se null'altro sente?* La verdad de tu brazo cambia lo
divino. Salir de sí con piedra contra el amor callado, lo
que no se termina para que haya perfección en la pérdida.
Huesos secos *de Dio formatti /* ojos sepultos antes de su
hora. Es el espíritu de una fruición de amor necesitado / la
parte superior de la inferior deja todo en su plato ofrecido.

CCXXXI

Severe light of stars / without virtue or specific task or compassion. The moon offers a ghost of a woman who once was a woman. Someone weeps in the viscera of desire. Campsites filled with footprints of having been refused access to the delegates of charity. The ground advances or rests with the zeal of stairs, the noncompliance of a mouth. In the night, finches that once knew how to sing.

CCXXXI

La luz severa de los astros / sin virtud ni obra particular ni compasión. La luna da un fantasma de mujer que fue mujer. Alguno llora en tripas del deseo. Campamentos con huellas de haber sido no admiten delegados de la caridad. El suelo avanza o se detiene en calentura de escalera, incumplimientos de una boca. En la noche hay jilgueros que sabían cantar.

CCXXXII

May there be worlds without ropes / without chains / their ruinous virtues have already choked too many / the tunics of blood / the kiss that kisses in sorrow / so many wars / delights broken. Globe where we are your woe / in some corner the debts of grace are borne. Love, linger yet before rising / there are no tongues to name you / the sheets are young at dawn.

CCXXXII

Haya universos sin cuerdas / sin cadenas / sus méritos de muerte ya ahorcaron demasiado / las túnicas de sangre / el beso que besa triste / las tantas guerras / las delicias quebradas. Mundo que somos tu miseria / en un rincón se aguantan las deudas de la gracia. No te levantes todavía amor / no hay lengua que te nombre / las sábanas son jóvenes al alba.

CCXXXIII

The liver they devour each day, reborn to be devoured again, wanders amid crossbred providence. In due time, first stage to last, it will boast the splendor of an eagle. Does it enter into flight with its glandular expertise? Does it store glycogens of deconstruction, contain the drainage of the executioner? It opens its eyes precisely when the winds sweep away the debris of the cosmos and a single naked word is gleaned. The arrows of Eros never strike the one they consume.

CCXXXIII

El hígado que cada día devoran y renace para ser devorado erra por mestizajes de la suerte. A su debido tiempo, del primer paso al último, tendrá fulgores de águila. ¿Entra al vuelo con su pericia glandular? ¿Almacena glucógenos de la deconstrucción, tiene drenajes del verdugo? Abre los ojos al instante en que los vientos barren desperdicios del cosmos y se ve una palabra desnuda. Las flechas de Eros nunca dan en el blanco del que comen.

CCXXXIV

If the questions were to end / to lose a child is nothing. The clients of borrowed love drown in equations for comfort. Neither the burning of the inner man / nor the warnings from the attending self / undo the customs of that deaf adventure. Rabbis / priests / mullahs / bound to immovable lunacies / blind to the shepherd's absence amid the undocumented sheep gone missing.

CCXXXIV

Si se acabaran las preguntas / perder un hijo es nada. Los clientes del amor prestado se hunden en matemáticas de la comodidad. Ni hombre interior quemando / ni advertencias del consigo mismo / deshacen las costumbres de esa aventura sorda. Rabinos / curas / mullahs / atados a locuras inmóviles / no ven la falta del pastor en las ovejas idas sin papeles.

CCXXXV

The brow's misfortune / thought it knew / its idle stars fled toward colorless skies. Fog ministers the exogenous territory, its sour and fleshless fear / it will grant them the dew and the rain of death. Eyes that shatter their sleep, where do they go? What backlight leaves them in the throes of death? Eros in the depths of the cave? The word will watch their backs, sometimes brandishing horror.

CCXXXV

Desdicha de la frente / creía saber / astros desocupados se le fueron a cielos sin color. La niebla cuida el fuero exógeno, su agrio temor sin carne / rocío y lluvia de la muerte les dará. ¿Adónde van los ojos que rompen su dormir? ¿Qué contraluz los deja en agonía? ¿Eros al fondo de la cueva? La palabra defiende su cintura hasta con el horror.

CCXXXVI

Sunup hushes, evening sears, between morning and night a
tendon is battered. The automaton is deprived of its letters,
the Delphi River runs slim, and eternity's dearth lies naked.
Dead stars insist on their light as if sworn to the perfection
of desire. Erotic relations climb the scales of arduous music
/ the immensity of being here unplundered. No one can
douse the fire that stood by action's vigils / opening / closing
/ the subsequent death.

CCXXXVI

La aurora ignora, la tarde arde, del día a la noche hay un
tendón golpeado. Le quitan letras al autómata, el río de
Delfos corre flaco y la pobreza de la eternidad está desnuda.
Astros muertos insisten en su luz como entregados a
perfección del deseo. La relación erótica sube escalas de
música difícil / la inmensidad del estar indespojada. Nadie
puede apagar el fuego que hubo en vigilias de la acción /
abrir / cerrar / la muerte próxima.

CCXXXVII

To lose an eye, a leg, a borrowed body, furrows of alcohol.
The terrestrial police lock up those suspected of unrewarded
loving / the light passing of a finch. How to understand
the fever of the bludgeons? Wait here, I'll be back, he said
/ beasts of a larger sort / calculations of iciness. The *portae
lucis* lost their power / who can cure the fear. Prosodic
accentuation feeds on saddened pages.

CCXXXVII

Perder un ojo, una pierna, cuerpo prestado, surcos del
alcohol. La policía terrestre encierra a sospechosos de
amar sin recompensa / el pasar leve de un jilguero. ¿Cómo
entender la fiebre de los palos? Esperá que yo vuelva, dijo
/ bestias mayores / cálculos del frío. La *portae lucis* perdió
electricidad / quién cura el miedo. La acentuación prosódica
come páginas tristes.

CCXXXVIII

You cleaved yourself from the worst / Chrétien de Troyes / from you / not *from that woman to whom you are subjected / who does not exist.* Within yourself whom could you have killed off. You invented tombs for love / the debacle / the doubt / Tristan Tzara loves you so much. Wrapped in paralytic rags / poverty did not defeat you / the piano that no longer resonates / theft from Chrétien. No one lends you dawns / abodes where everything lasts so long. Now, in Mexico City / your music / the nerves you rile / the fabrication of blessings / the question who am I.

CCXXXVIII

Te separaste de lo peor / Chrétien de Troyes / de vos / no *de aquella a la que estás sujeto / la que no existe.* En vos mismo a quién ibas a matar. Inventaste sepulcros de amor / del se acabó / la duda / Tristán Tzara te quiere mucho. Envuelto en trapos paralíticos / no te venció la carestía / el piano que no suena / robo de Chrétien. Nadie te presta amaneceres / moradas donde todo dura mucho. Ahora en México, D.F. / tu música / los nervios que encrespás / la construcción de dichas / la pregunta quién soy.

CCXXXIX

What is neither light nor circle nor star on a happy day / heavy-laden takes flight. It remains in the fever-swollen hand that touched melancholy without mourning, the impossibility of the sparrow, the intercourse with furious battles. Memory snags its garb in ire's debris. The third one there between the dead and the longsuffering never shows his face. Sure of the fulfillment of their duty, vagaries return evil for goodness. Love's decrees beg for the woman who can conjoin the syllables.

CCXXXIX

Lo que no es luz ni círculo ni estrella en un día feliz / cargado vuela. Queda en la mano túmida de fiebre que tocó melancolías sin duelo, la imposibilidad del gorrión, las relaciones con batallas furiosas. La memoria desgarra sus vestidos en desperdicios de la cólera. El tercero entre el muerto y el doliente nunca muestra la cara. Seguras del deber cumplido, vaguedades devuelven mal por bien. Las ordenanzas del amor mendigan la mujer que une sílabas.

CCXL

Smash the world to pieces, devour their innards, the false façades, strip them of their never. These are the demands of fervor, of hopeful blood, of indignation left hanging out to dry. Why do those opposed to the poem that fondles its impossible tend to prosper? Rooms where love was quick, leaving a town in the four walls of an instant. Thus and so to be born in the gunpowder of the clandestinities that devours them.

CCXL

Romper el mundo en pedacitos, devorarles la entraña, los falsos continentes, desarroparles el jamás. Esto exigen la fiebre, la sangre esperadora, la indignación que cuelgan a secar. ¿Por qué prosperan los opuestos al poema que roza su imposible? Cuartos donde el amor estuvo rápido and deja una ciudad en las cuatro paredes del instante. Así sería nacer en pólvoras de clandestinidad que la devoran.

CCXLI

The phenomena of deconstruction go mute on torturing nights. And what would guilt be without wings soaring in the past, a body of annunciation prior to departing? Where to store poorly borne magnitudes within one rifle round? The flesh is searching for transparencies in a corner of forget-me-nots. Goodness is suffering from evil in the studies of joy.

For Hugo Gutiérrez Vega

CCXLI

Fenómenos de la deconstrucción son callados en noches que torturan. ¿Y qué sería una culpa sin alas volando en el pasado, cuerpo de anunciación antes de irse? ¿Dónde guardar envergaduras mal sostenidas en un tiro? La carne busca transparencias en un rincón del nomeolvides. El bien está enfermo del mal en los estudios de la dicha.

A Hugo Gutiérrez Vega

CCXLII

They want to underrate, to undercut the airs of levitation
as if it were mere accident / a blemish / a calamity. And
the rose, the animals of desire, the quiver of the hand on
a moon, where will they live? Moments of misery coupled
in the waters of flight, the I believes it is other and declines
truth's table scraps in the estuaries of the tongue.

CCXLII

Quieren arrebajar, abajar, los aires de la levitación como si
fuera un accidente / un punto negro / una desgracia. ¿Y
dónde vivirán la rosa, los animales del deseo, el temblor de
la mano en una luna? Instantes de la miseria acaballada en
aguas de la huida, el yo cree que es otro, declina sobras de la
verdad en los esteros de la lengua.

CCXLIII

To your health, kisses that go to and fro, open to blind
tutelage. How many women in dressless lives? Daughters
/ sons / burnt in malignant bane / less than being /
catastrophes of the fist. The word thaws and wets the upper
layers / splashing the fretwork of the void. As for birds,
nothing. Intention neither locates nor creates joy / under the
sun's squanderings, being-here badgers. On death's balcony
fingers appear that were stirring in nights of revolvers and
dread and dreams of truth and offerings of heady thyme.

CCXLIII

Salud, besos que van para otro lado y se abren a tutelas de
ciego. Cuánta mujer en vidas sin vestido. Hijas / hijos /
quemados en pestes malas / menos del ser / catástrofes del
puño. La palabra se descongela, moja el encima / salpica
encajes del vacío. De los pájaros, nada. La intención no
encuentra ni hace dicha, estar insiste bajo derroches del
sol. Al balcón de la muerte se asoman dedos que hubo en
noches de revolver y miedo y sueños de verdad y entregas
del tomillo en pleno aroma.

CCXLIV

Swerves, dour dog days, abandonment of clemency, dens
of never, disciples of dread, rootless passions, pitiless wars,
I without me, diseases of the spirit, hemorrhages of horror,
enemies of the dead, armbands that have fled, may it be
known forever, rummaging through entrails, childhood
cast in lead, the favors of forty nights, haunted mountains,
conceivable conclusions of happiness, BA 5 a.m., elixir
of the message, hallway occasions, epistolaries, maritime
nightmares and all that. That.

CCXLIV

Derrapes, ásperas canículas, deserciones de la clemencia,
antros del nunca, discípulos del miedo, pasiones sin raíz,
guerras crudas, el yo sin yo, achaques del espíritu, derrames
del espanto, enemigos del muerto, brazaletes fugados, que
se sepas por siempre, rebusques de la entraña, niñez fundida
en plomo, favores de cuarenta noches, montañas poseídas,
se diera por feliz, cinco de la mañana de Buenos Aires, elixir
del mensaje, las ocasiones de pasillo, epístolas, pesadumbres
del mar y eso. Eso.

CCXLV

The bird from Tonalá is singing on the platter / never exchanging one loss for another. Thus destiny discovers its roots, Lesbos maidens in long white tunics / may death be mistaken. Wine's wanderers have heavy-bodied instruments. Definitions of the strings, incoherencies of a unity that parleys. Its appetite is humble, fleeing from the chimera, lingering in its passion, shredding clouds and sensing palpitations, powders, times when love is daubed with its broken edges.

For Paola

CCXLV

El pájaro de Tonalá canta en el plato / no cambia una pérdida por otra. Así el destino encuentra orígenes, las muchachas de Lesbos con largas túnicas, y que la muerte se equivoque. Los viajeros del vino tienen instrumentos con cuerpo. Definiciones de las cuerdas, incoherencias de su unidad que parla. Su apetito es humilde, huye de la quimera, se queda en su pasión, rompe nubes y pasan palpitaciones, pólvoras, las veces que el amor se unta con sus orillas rotas.

A Paola

CCXLVI

Where do they keep vigil over bread and onions on the stone slabs of hunger? Fully conscious of the cruelty of sweetness. Merciless, a tarnished Eros befriends his desert / echelons / purples / puckers in used furniture / poems without lye / what would they eat of us? Hospitals remedy semantic deviations and their fragrance drifts into a void, never to be discovered. The shriek annihilates the snakes all around, perplexing prize for distracted I/s.

CCXLVI

¿Dónde velan el pan y la cebolla en baldosa del hambre? Conocen la crueldad de la dulzura. El Eros deslucido se amiga con su desierto sin piedad / escalafones / púrpuras / pliegues de mueble usado / poemas sin cal viva / ¿qué nos quieren comer? Los hospitales curan desvaríos semánticos y su fragancia va a un abismo donde no la hallarán. El llanto acaba con serpientes alrededor, trofeo turbio de yo/ es distraídos.

CCXLVII

Infinitely thread-worn words leave us quaking, they gaze at the cloud-mantled moon. The draining flow of the ego / the I in its storm, and amid the smoke suppositions grow / stars the hand cannot grasp. Pointless to pursue the sky's lightning bolt. And the fealty of forsakenness.

CCXLVII

La palabra caduca al infinito deja temblores, ve la luna con nubes que la tapan. El fluido del ego / yo se agota en su tormenta, alrededor del humo crecen suposiciones / astros que la mano no agarra. Inútil es perseguir al relámpago que pasa. Y la fidelidad del desamparo.

CCXLVIII

To flee from the scene / mathematical recommendations / trope / *trópos* / windmills of ire / head of the household / it will take your women / a hundred / a thousand years / nonexistent nights. Resistance defeats / orphan bones / cold parts of the pantry that do not gel / felled smiles / duties behind the offer. When will the wise rocamboles appear / the spear's chorus / a blind spot / the broom / the copper bedspread? They erect ruins of living / insouciant cities / cordoned off / arrival that never came.

For Ignacio Uranga

CCXLVIII

Huir del cuadro / las recomendaciones matemáticas / tropo / *trope* / molinos de la ira / la frente del hogar / cien / mil años / tomará tus mujeres / las noches no sidas. La resistencia vence / huesos huérfanos / partes frías de la bodega sin cuajar / sonrisas cáidas / responsabilidades de la oferta. ¿Cuándo vendrán rocámbulos despiertos / los coros de la lanza / punta ciega / la escoba / las sábanas de cobre? Construyen ruinas de vivir / ciudades sin fulgor / cerradas / venir que nunca fue.

A Ignacio Uranga

CCXLIX

Hamlet, once lost, to be or not to be is not to be. The alcazar of a sorrowful Apollonian duel mantles the trees of every death, seven dwellings exist in the vicinity of the hyacinth. With no mother now, how will the forget-you-not water make it grow? Love / they're knocking at the door. The I runs to hide / the woman speaking has departed with flowers on empty balconies.

CCXLIX

Hamlet perdido, ser o no ser es ser no ser. El alcázar del duelo apolíneo despliega mantos sobre los árboles de cada muerto, siete moradas viven en vecindades del jacinto. Sin madre ahora, ¿cómo lo hará crecer el agua noteolvido? Amor / golpean sus puertas. El yo se esconde / habla la que se fue con flores en terrazas vacías.

CCL

Dread is oblivious to the suns of night / distanced bodies / the departed in his heights. The deceased returns to this abandonment. The mechanisms of the hyperboles fall silent in swiftness / wines you are bound to drink / public disgrace. Insanities occupy a poor man's plate. Discordances negate the five tomes of waiting / departing is not a lifelong sorrow. They've left / spending their brokenness in seasons of dog bites / hushing like the sparks of a diamond. Wood / wind / flooding love / pageants that do not parade / being-here / erased by truths.

CCL

El espanto olvida soles de la noche / los cuerpos distanciados / el ido en sus alturas. El muerto vuelve a su abandono. Los mecanismos de las hipérboles callan en velocidades / vinos que has de beber / las ignominias públicas. Hay locura en el plato de un pobre. Discordancias niegan los cinco tomos de la espera / irse no pesará toda la vida. Se fueron / pasan su rotez por estaciones de la mordedura / callan como destellos de un diamante. Montes / vientos / amor en los derrames / cortejos que no marchan / estar / verdades que lo borran.

CCLI

Spectacles of the I have a shade of gray that none applaud / unplumbable moans / things that occur behind our backs without light or compassion. Cut and unbind / the snakes' hissing is unbearable. Soul they attack / clockless wings / soaring / soaring.

CCLI

Los espectáculos del yo tienen un gris que nadie aplaude / los ayes insondables / lo que sucede a espaldas sin luz ni compasión. Cortar y desatar / no se aguantan silbidos de la víbora. Alma que atacan / alas sin reloj / vuelan / vuelan.

CCLII

Chance has domes / eludes doctorates, fabrications that thread by thread renounce it. Nothing to do with mathematics, schemes of evil / goodness / effects that complicate its pithiness. It sidesteps the fire of refined young women / scions of the damask rose / the elaborate coincidence / it sketches no designs / men of license / it comes and goes / straight from night. Victorious in the mode of I will fall in love / I will hate / I will die / it soars in its uncertain and cloudless sky with neither sleepwalkers nor signs of nothingness.

CCLII

El azar tiene cúpulas, elude doctorados, tramas que hilo por hilo lo reniegan. Nada que ver con matemáticas, complots de la maldad / bondad / efectos que confunden su sazón. Sortea el incendio de las muchachas finas / vástagos del rosal / casualidades trabajadas / no traza planes / hombres permitidos / viene y se va / derecho de la noche. Vence al estilo me enamoré / odiaré / moriré / vuela en su cielo incierto sin nubes ni sonámbulos ni indicios de la nada.

CCLIII

Is it thread / cord / rope? Endless crimson / feathers / apart from the wine? Years traipsing lands beneath a double sun / ineluctable autumns / images of a salty climb. Manuals for rites are mindless of good fortune / they parch the rains' very breasts. The hunted boar rootles yet. Every animal finds its end / homeless livers / petunias in an envelope / the circuit's resolutions. Where will the holm oaks of vision go / far from fading dogs.

CCLIII

¿Es hilo / cuerda / soga? ¿Carmín que no termina / plumas / amén del vino? Años pisando tierras bajo el doble sol / otoños sin remedio / imágenes que van a sal arriba. Los manuales del rito no cuidan suertes buenas / secan los senos de la lluvia. El jabalí cazado hunde el hocico. Todo animal se acaba / hígados sin casa / petunias en un sobre / resoluciones del circuito. Adónde irán encinos de la visión / lejos de perros que se apagan.

CCLIV

Steps echo in the house of the new instrument. What is it doing with its vestibule now sealed off? Form and matter have potions / feet falling on the blades of wind / systems of pride. The grandeur of the swan will turn to dew when it dies / pleasure's awe / too scant for cleansing the world. There are strings scorn never plucks / its tutelary stealth closes doors to the tiny corpse bereft of epitaphs.

CCLIV

Pasos resuenan en la casa del instrumento nuevo. ¿Qué hace con su vestíbulo cerrado? La forma y la materia tienen brebajes / pisan el filo de los vientos / sistemas del orgullo. La grandeza del cisne será rocío cuando muera / asombro del placer / no alcanzará para lavar el mundo. Hay cuerdas que el desprecio no toca / su sigilo guardián cierra puertas al muertito sin nota necrológica.

CCLV

They inaugurate barbarities of consolation. Landless benevolence displays its demon / its frailty / masks / rags / chests / navels painfully included. The time has come to unhitch horses / sweet bucking / disasters of the disaster. Hurried outings discover scenes of heaping plates beyond / bottles of grapes with nowhere to nestle. Grandeurs of the pulp explode / motifs of a vibrant midnight. Inevitably the eyelids close / paying for sleep with centuries.

CLV

Fundan barbaridades del consuelo. Muestra su diablo la bondad sin tierra / su desamparo / máscaras / harapos / pechos / ombligos van a penas. Es tiempo de abrir caballos / corcovos dulces / desastres del desastre. Viajes relámpago descubren escenas de plato lleno afuera / botellas de uva sin regazo. Estallan grandezas de la pulpa / motivos de medianoche viva. Los párpados se cierran sin remedio / pagan siglos al sueño.

CCLVI

The forbearance of barrens is tarnished by the word barrens. The beloved sleeps in the hearts of tired bliss / time's tests / stars that come and go with their wounds. She mounts with immaculate tack / times long gone / summits of the face she wrote as a child / the future above and beyond being. From her, fleeting breezes / the reunion of being-here with her non-presence / celebrations in a glass of water. Raindrops / she says.

CCLVI

Las paciencias del páramo deslucen en la palabra páramo. La amada duerme en núcleos de la dicha cansada / exámenes del tiempo / astros que van y vienen con heridas. Monta en arnés sin mácula / tiempos que fueron / cumbres del rostro que escribió de niña / el porvenir por encima del ser. Le salen brisas breves / el encuentro de estar con su no estar / celebraciones en un vaso de agua. Agüita / dice.

CCLVII

Short is the day when fury subsides / the act does not fit its mystery. Passion offers up its ashes like doomsday septicity. The bone sustains its beauty / surviving the time of the primordial worm / in centuries-old paintings the skull is clean / perfect / white / no rot or ruin. No thing other remains from the pennoning dawn / flesh aflame in the missives of desire / misery of its synthesis.

For Lisa Bradford

CCLVII

Corto es el día en que el furor se acaba / el acto no entra en su misterio. La pasión ofrece su ceniza como contagio del final. El hueso sostiene a la belleza / sobrevive al tiempo del anélido / la calavera es limpia en cuadros de hace siglos / perfecta / blanca / sin putrefacción. Nada otra cosa queda del aladeo del alba / carne que ardió en mensajes del deseo / miseria de su síntesis.

A Lisa Bradford

CCLVIII

Charles, return with your impurity so everything might change / petite virtú / the meanness of this patience. Jarry, return with your son-slaying pistol. And may others return / Mamnermus in lusty dreams of horses / *tender thorns* of Rudel / the declining sunset of Donne / Hölderlin with his desk. End this nightmare / rend the rhythmless nets / the world's poverty / its reptile in disguise. Sing once again against / filth that wounds the night.

For Ivan Trejo

CCLVIII

Charles volvé con tu impureza para que todo cambie / la pequeña virtud / la mezquindad de esta paciencia. Jarry volvé con tu pistola matahijos. Y que vuelvan Mimnermo ávido sueño de caballos / *espinos suaves* de Rudel / el ocaso empinado de John Donne / Hölderlin con su pupitre. Acaben esta pesadilla / rompan redes sin ritmo / la pobreza del mundo / su reptil disfrazado. Canten de nuevo contra / suciedades que hieren a la noche.

A Iván Trejo

CCLIX

To unstitch unities / the mesmerisms of being-here / the more of less / antilogies of haste / the word / abodes of horror / intentional clarity / anthologies of the past / loves dethroned / the word / zeros of hatred / conclusions on the bone / accounts of the mistaken / tables of truth / the word / economic heavens / dispersion of the paradox / impoverished hands / there is no backward / the word / deserts in sight / withering waits / underlying bodies / the word / errors of the consequence / dreams that were two / died / the word words / the word /

For Jorge Boccanera

CCLIX

Descoser unidades / los mesmerismos del estar / el más del menos / antilogías del apuro / la palabra / las residencias del horror / la claridad a propósito / antologías del pasado / amores destituidos / la palabra / ceros del odio / dictámenes del hueso / las cuentas del equívoco / tablas de la verdad / la palabra / los cielos económicos / desbandes de la paradoja / manos pobres / no hay atrás / la palabra / desiertos a la vista / esperas mustias / cuerpos debajo / la palabra / errores de la trascendencia / sueños que fueron dos / murieron / la palabra palabra / la palabra /

A Jorge Boccanera

CCLX

The shudder of a turtledove shatters similarities. Being-here. Where do the exchanges between good and evil in the passive organs finally wind up? The I assays deceit in the restlessness of itself / papers / salvaging the flaw. The city spills forth / trees / laundry hanging on the line / tiny creatures on the corner. No one poses questions / when the river runs clear, there emerge instructions from the one who was / names he never had / phosphorescence never seen. The tongue lowers the curtain / there is no applause / there are children / dying of hunger.

CCLX

El repelús de la torcaza rompe las semejanzas. Estar. ¿A dónde van los intercambios del bien y el mal en órganos pasivos? El yo practica trampas en la inquietud de sí / papeles / rescates de la falta. La ciudad se derrama / árboles / ropa al secado / animalitos de la esquina. Nadie pregunta nada / cuando se aclara el río caen las instrucciones del que fue / los nombres que no tuvo / fosforescencias nunca habidas. La lengua baja el telón / no hay aplausos / hay niños / mueren de hambre.

CCLXI

Douse the light, dousing, dousing all, tombolo of death /
I have come and I am leaving. Are we only able to expose
the lair of things lost, old parchment, the sudden shocks of
desire? The body sinters mistakes / firing like a kiln. Passion
stomps on what has ended / pillows that trembled / circuits
of closed vision.

CCLXI

Apagar, apagar, apagar, tómbolas de la muerte / vine y me
voy. ¿Sólo se puede desabrigar el escondite de la pérdida,
pliegues viejos, los sobresaltos del deseo? El cuerpo cuece
errores / iguala oficios del hornillo. La pasión pisa lo que
terminó / almohadas que temblaron / circuitos de la visión
cerrada.

CCLXII

To be / to be here / joined in ontological distances / the being / immobile thing / dead many philosophical bloods ago. Does being-here serve hors d'oeuvres at ceremonious intervals? What root joins them by separating them? Is the rose rose or does it derive from the rose? Silence crumbles into midnight liquors. Oh, night, night that would not be without you / being-here in you like a slumbering skylark.

CCLXII

El ser / estar / unidos en distancias ontológicas / el ser / cosa inmóvil / muerto hace mucha sangre filosófica. ¿El estar sirve sus platillos en estadios? ¿Y qué raíz los une separándolos? / ¿La rosa es rosa o viene de la rosa? Se derrumban callares en los alcoholes de la noche. Oh, noche, noche que no podría ser sin vos / estar en vos como alondra dormida.

CCLXIII

Labyrinths of man / woman / swift dawns. What tinder feeds their fires? The breathing of sweet eyelids? The spirit ropes the animals of need. It exhumes emanations from the bedrooms of the abyss / the remnants of April / chimeras that terrorize / returning to twice-told love. In the sprawling whys and wherefores there are trees unknown / barristers asking questions / a woman in cold sweats come midnight.

CCLXIII

Los laberintos hombre / mujer / albas veloces. ¿Qué madera alimenta su fuego? ¿El aliento de los dulces párpados? El espíritu voltea animales de la necesidad. Cava vahos en cuartos del vacío / restos de abril / quimeras que aterrizan / volver a amor por vez segunda. En el despliegue del por qué hay árboles desconocidos / notarios que preguntan / una mujer que suda frio a medianoche.

CCLXIV

To live a bit more, *forza del tuo valore* / final proof /
luxurious ambition. To snuff out with a wink histories to
come / unfordable. Who is working the broncos in the
underbelly of what never occurred? To leave the invisible
ajar / forests of the conscience / fleeting regions / remnants
of saying and doing / inside out. He who digs will discover
unities / the scissors with the cut / the raucous river with the
drought / the murderer with the murdered / permission for
the tragedy to end with a certain glow.

CCLXIV

Vivir un poco más, *forza del tuo valore* / prueba final / lujosa
pretensión. Apagar con un guiño historias que vendrán /
no traspasables. ¿Quién labra potros en el envés de lo que
no pasó? Entreabrir lo invisible / montes de la conciencia /
regiones breves / restos de dicho y hecho / los reversos. El
que cava descubre unidades / la tijera con el cortado / el río
audible con la seca / el asesino con el asesinado / permisos
para que la desgracia sea con un cierto fulgor.

CCLXV

Roses on the balcony across the way / jasmines bantering
in choral splendor. Where will their aromas go if not to the
loss that is never lost? Morning burnishes their liaison with
upper case letters / binding habits / absences that do not
depart. Extensions of suffering / challenges of being-here /
belated discoveries.

For Ignacio Uranga

CCLXV

Las rosas del balcón contrario / jazmines conversados por
fulgores cantables. ¿A dónde irá su aroma sino a la pérdida
que no se pierde? Las mañanas pulen su relación con las
mayúsculas / hábitos de lo anudado / ausencias que no
se van. Las extensiones del padecer / osadías de estar /
descubrimientos tarde.

A Ignacio Uranga

CCLXVI

One hour is worth everything that ever was / by its side live pieces of the struggle / vibrations of the incandescence / death lying in wait. The visits from noises that leave you sleepless / errors / Hartmann von Aue with *sidelong glances from the ladies*. The mortars of the softest love pulverize the unquestioned core / the fable of I am able. Loneliness wraps itself around the bone, tenacious as lengthy pleasure.

CCLXVI

Una hora vale todo lo que hubo / pedazos de la lucha viven a su costado / vibraciones de la incandescencia / la muerte enfrente. Las visitas del ruido que no deja dormir / errores / Hartam von Aue *mirado de soslayo por las damas*. Los morteros del amor más suave destrozan el interior creído / la fábula del puedo. Hay soledad alrededor del hueso que resiste como goce largo.

CCLXVII

The foot is capable of crossing the forest / never entering glaciers of salvation / breeze without baptism / scarecrows of the scarlet purple. It walks to its heartbeat / bolstering the roof of preparations / flights of the nerve / never-ending payment of the doubt. An accordion sings to the Gulf of Mexico when seeking perfection / psalming its extremes. Night will arrive, deferential to its music / the real exposed to realities / naked rock / its invisibility.

CCLXVII

El pie puede cruzar el bosque / no entra a glaciares de la salvación / la brisa sin bautismo / los espantajos de la púrpura. Camina su latido / refuerza el techo de la preparación / vuelos del nervio / pagos eternos de la duda. Un acordeón canta al Golfo de México cuando desea perfecciones / salmodia sus extremos. Vendrá la noche obediente a su música / el real expuesto a realidades / roca desnuda / su invisible.

CCLXVIII

This cricket in my hand, which I instantly fall in love with, tells me his topcoat is last night. No moment is today when set alongside the body that adds up each one. Cool inside, familiar, and death, how it dissembles. The word disappears, the cricket sings, and on the street one sees the mirrors of misery, joys shipwrecked in the bud, assassins of the paper verb. Time winds its clock with buckskin mares tied round the neck.

CCLXVIII

Este grillo en la mano que amo instantáneamente me dice que su abrigo es anoche. Cada momento no es hoy al lado del cuerpo que lo suma. Fresco ahí, reconocible, la muerte que cómo disimula. La palara desaparece, el grillo canta y en la calle se ven miserias del cristal, dichas que naufragaron jóvenes, asesinos del verbo papel. El tiempo da cuerda a su reloj con yeguas bayas alrededor del cuello.

CCLXIX

Freefall into receptacles of fear / blood / bleeding. Lowercase phases / schemes worth nothing / not even the genesis of forms. Each semantic unity manipulates questions / ignorance / water ablaze. The theologian's bazars are washed into silent seas / analogies of the beginning. Let the lightning bolts of the syncope explode / the lie of savage historicity / hand exposed / inequities of love.

CCLXIX

Caída en receptáculos del miedo / sangre / sangra. Estadios de minúsculas / ardides que no sirven / ni génesis de formas. Cada unidad semántica manipula preguntas / las ignorancias / aguas con fuego. Se derraman las tiendas del teólogo en mares silenciosos / comparaciones del comienzo. Estallen los refuciles de la síncopa / la mentira de la historicidad salvaje / la mano al aire / injusticias de amor.

CCLXX

Do not expect the defeated man to hush / to stop loving / stop wiping the moisture from his lumber with questions from the ravaged eye. The flesh on the bone learns to share subsequent songs / the trees of a tree / the throats of a nest / morning sores / wounded accounts. Who will pay for night? Scents from the shore tell him what needs to be done.

For Geneviève Fabry

CCLXX

No esperen que el derrotado calle / deje de amar / sacar humedad de su madera con preguntas del ojo aplastado. La carne alrededor del hueso aprende a convidar las canciones siguientes / los árboles de un árbol / las gargantas de un nido / llagas de la mañana / las cuentas de la herida. ¿Quién pagará la noche? Aromas de la orilla le dicen lo que hay que hacer.

A Geneviève Fabry

CCLXXI

Within the womb of the line, a woman is lost in dreams,
crossing saturations of listening / accidents by proxy / the
warmth of the bed. Where do her parts roam before dawn?
What does it matter that she hate the day's betrayals / rotting
rancor / *the foul carcass* sung by Baudelaire. Oh, father of
afterward / homeland gone / heart wanting no succor. He
amassed words so they might relate the labor pains of death.

CCLXXI

En las entrañas de la línea sueña una mujer. Cruza
saturaciones del escuche / accidentes de la procuración / el
calor de la cama. ¿A dónde van sus partes hasta el amanecer?
Qué importa si odia las traiciones del día / rencores que se
pudren / *la carroña infame* que cantó Baudelaire. Oh, padre
del después / el pago ido / corazón que no quiso socorro.
Ganó palabras para que dijeran los partos de la muerte.

CCLXXII

From poetry to poem / to go / how / its current leaves a piece amid the rices of the wedding / its dayest moment / to black ink thereafter. Mute womb / gem left in its gemness / what can I make of you in me / dazzler. You never leave your house / you whirl about / paining like a red-hot iron. Serving your wine, the myrtle you planted so the impossible might return.

For José Ángel Leyva

CCLXXII

De la poesía al poema / ir / cómo / su corriente deja un pedazo en los arroces de la boda / su momento más día / después a tinta negra. Entraña muda / joya quedada en su joyez / qué hago de vos en mí / deslumbradora. No salís de tu casa / girás alrededor / dolés como hierro candente. Sirve tu vino el mirto que sembraste para que vuelva lo imposible.

A José Ángel Leyva

CCLXXIII

The fog that erases the tower knows its fate. It raises
unfurlings of reality in its tuneless source, closing notebooks
of maybes. Splendid affair / muting its second motif in the
human season of harrowing. The one / being-here and
death take a sidelong glance at their true malaise, a missive
in the saddest look of a dog.

For Juan Marsé

CCLXXIII

La niebla que borra a la torre conoce su destino. Alza
desdoblamientos de la realidad en su cauce sin música,
cierra cuadernos de lo que puede ser. Bella cosa / calla su
segundo motivo en la estación humana del desgarro. El
uno / estar y la muerte ven con ojos oblicuos su verdadera
enfermedad, una carta en la mirada más triste de un perro.

A Juan Marsé

CCLXXIV

Inking their distance, the preludes of the how / the no-language of wait-for-me / the street of children entrapped. Irún / you shall not pass / said the walls / the father's stare / the silence at the table / Godless prayers / wastelands of warnings. Out of what wood can loss be carved? To sleep without changing the date / nocturnal remains sizzle in the soup / the persistence of desire / the firebrands of sense. The vanquished lost his eternity in the rocks where an ibis once stood / the river that cleansed the moon / the stature of a diamond.

For Antonio Gamoneda

CCLXXIV

Los preludios del cómo entintan su distancia / el no lenguaje del espérame / la calle de los niños tocados. Irún / no pasarán / decían las paredes / la mirada del padre / el silencio en la mesa / rezos sin Dios / páramos del presagio. ¿De qué madera hacer lo que se pierde? Dormir sin cambiar el día / restos nocturnos que arden en la sopa / la persistencia del deseo / los fierros del sentido. El derrotado perdió su eternidad en piedras donde una garza estuvo / el río que lavó a la luna / las estaturas del diamante.

A Antonio Gamoneda

CCLXXV

In traveling to words vacant domains are left within. When will they lose their limits? The courage to look one's self in the face is filthy with fears / salaries of being-here / greenrooms of performance. In which pit / how can one dig to make it become? The opposite of what we are closes doors / traps / the Greek who saw black laurels. There are wretched waters that should never be repeated / beds that return / underbellies of bonfires / ephemeral masks for oneself only / bottles received by no sea / the deer's eye that will blossom in its with-me-ness.

For Arturo Rivera

CCLXXV

Irse a palabra deja adentro territorios vaciados. ¿Cuándo serán sin límites? El coraje de mirarse a sí mismo está sucio de miedos / los sueldos del estar / camarines de la representación. ¿Hasta qué fondo / cómo cavar para que sea? Lo contrario que somos cierra puertas / trampas / el griego que vio laureles negros. Hay aguas míseras que no debieran repetirse / camas que vuelven / entresijos de hogueras / máscaras breves de uno para uno / las botellas que ningún mar recibe / el ojo de venado que será flor en su conmigo.

A Arturo Rivera

CCLXXVI

I hear poems that will never be written / their flight hovers above my motionless hand / pleasure of their dissatisfaction. How to touch the bristling numbers / the past yet to come / repetitions of desire? Arid / arrogant / impossibility leaves faces in a corner now lost. The endowments of silence reveal its underbelly in let me be yours / may you be mine. The bone possesses tunics it will lose without ever having seen you / no one can catch you, heartling. Welcome to the night where your never greens in being.

CCLXXVI

Oigo poemas que no se escribirán / su vuelo pasa sobre la mano quieta / goce de su insatisfacción. ¿Cómo tocar los números que erizan / el pasado que va a venir / repeticiones del deseo? Seca / airosa / la imposibilidad deja rostros en un rincón perdido. Las dotaciones del silencio muestran su envés en déjame ser tuyo / que mía seas. El hueso tiene túnicas que perderá sin verte / nadie te atrapa, corazona. Bienvenida a la noche donde verdea tu nunca en ser.

CCLXXVII

The reproach there lounging with red pajamas in a bed of love / lies. Tensions of the with / of the for / of the non-progressing hate / stopovers of the instant / brushes with death. What collapses in a contract? Listening to the music of self-suspicion / the hours of celebration / the flashes of the absent place. Smoke from the past spews into the body's parts / imperfect confusions / the sorrows they fabricate. Behind the fear stands another fear / awake / needles at the ready. The two spheres of being-here are acquainted with their impossible. Nothing remains without travelling to the pieces it cannot conjoin.

For George-Henri Melanotte

CCLXXVII

El reproche apoyado con un pijama rojo en un lecho de amor / miente. Tensiones del con / del por / del odio sin progreso / parajes del instante / los roces de la muerte. ¿Qué se derrumba en un contrato? Oír la música del sospechar de sí / las horas de la fiesta / los resplandores del lugar ausente. En las partes del cuerpo se derraman los humos del pasado / las confusiones imperfectas / los sufrimientos que fabulan. Detrás del miedo hay otro miedo / despierto / con agujas. Las dos esferas del estar conocen su imposible. Nada queda sin irse a los pedazos que no puede reunir.

A George-Henri Melanotte

CCLXXVIII

In the meandering of what's been learned there's a market where nothing is sold. The ruins speak to the next person, his failure that maims decisions as regards going back. Think about it (ponder that) in the sparks the stone in / cites.

CCLXXVIII

En la deambulación de lo aprendido está el mercado donde se vende nada. Las ruinas hablan al sujeto ulterior, su fracaso que hiere las decisiones del regreso. Pensalo (piénsalo) en resplandores que la piedra con / vida.

CCLXXIX

Which key did you use to open your door? In the shade of which tree did you discover / Apollinaire / countries of a decency you'd never seen? So sweet you were with your skull cracked open by desires more powerful than a howitzer / you raised a cow that proffered shade to incurable breasts. Oh, so gently, entering yourself to lose yourself again.

CCLXXIX

¿Con qué llave abriste tu puerta? ¿Bajo qué árbol encontraste / Apollinaire / países de la bondad que jamás viste? Dulce eras con la cabeza partida por deseos más fuertes que un obús / criabas una vaca que daba sombra a pechos incurables. Oh, suave, entrándote a vos mismo para perderte de una vez.

CCLXXX

Today hurts, no distraction possible / neither the bird that once consoled consoles him now / nor what will be was / nor sources for pentameters / nor prizes for tenderness / nor world rotting away / nor gunshots that did not in fact wound him / nor the polenta of his childhood / nor fear around the corner / nor scars in the hidden crook / nor tears for what has not been / ramblings through the beloved landscape in his heart today.

CCLXXX

Hoy duele sin distracción posible, ni el pájaro que consolaba lo consuela / ni lo que será fue / ni fuentes del endecasílabo / ni premios de la ternura / ni el mundo que se pudre / ni los balazos que no lo hirieron de verdad / ni la polenta de la infancia / ni el miedo a la vuelta de la esquina / ni cicatrices de rincón oculto / ni llorar por lo no sido / las vueltas del paisaje amado hoy en el corazón.

CCLXXXI

I quarry myself to stop covering you up with more visions of your long coat. A blink lasts forever when the being is severed from itself in soundless flights. Still free between cement walls and lye / hurled to never becoming certitude.

For Marcelo

CCLXXXI

Me cavo para no encubrirte más con visiones de tu abrigo largo. Un parpadeo dura mucho cuando se aparta el ser de sí en vuelos sin rumor. Libre aún entre muros de cemento y cal viva / arrojado a que nunca fueras certidumbre.

A Marcelo

CCLXXXII

The din of continuation marks every January / it hinders wings, voices that fly off, words never used / a woman's clothing falls in a dead tongue. Irritations of an impotent bird crinkle skies that do not dream the dream of confinement / the demands of the eyelids / the leap into the green nothingness. Death answers with ruptures and the letters from the verbs of passion bear no postage. In rebar bracelets May beloved above all. The sentinel shuts the gate / tiring of enraptured acts in freezing chambers.

CCLXXXII

Estrépitos de la continuación marcan cualquier enero / impiden alas, voces que van, palabras nunca usadas / cae la ropa de mujer en una lengua muerta. Irritaciones del pájaro incapaz arrugan cielos que no sueñan el sueño del confín / las exigencias de los párpados / el salto hacia la nada verde. La muerte contesta con rupturas y las cartas del verbo pasional no tienen estampillas. Mayo querido sobre sí con pulseras de fierro. El centinela cierra el portón / se cansa de los actos absortos en cámaras heladas.

CCLXXXIII

Which key is it? Who is blocking the entrance to autumn beds where evil snuffs out their countries? Meandering around what was lost one finds the market where nothing is sold. / the failure that maims decisions as regards going back. / persecutions of the past against filthy disguises / words without ashes / boxed up breath / and no one no one no one.

CCLXXXIII

¿Con qué llave se abren? ¿Quién impide la entrada a lechos del otoño donde el mal apaga sus países? En la deambulación de lo perdido está el mercado donde se vende nada. / el fracaso que hiere las decisiones del regreso. / persecuciones del pasado contra disfraces sucios / palabras sin cenizas / respiraciones encajadas / y nadie nadie nadie.

CCLXXXIV

Dock Sud, a bitter port, the question that remained there and still remains. It ties up night with ropes / a vision that rips open what is real / the infinite begins and ends in an instant. Wounds of the flesh / bones beneath a painful downpour / decisions that could bear no more.

CCLXXXIV

El sur, un puerto amargo, la pregunta que allí quedó y se queda. Ata con sogas a la noche / una visión que rasga el real / el infinito empieza y termina en un instante. Heridas de la carne / huesos bajo una lluvia dolorosa / las decisiones que no podían más.

CCLXXXV

What must be spoken goes unspoken and floats in quagmires of global pomp. There, a wee bit below, where a star manufactures Parnassian steeds, they dig up tears, wars, sorrows that once existed, becoming brothers in chasmal climes. Where does the failure of those innards fit / ready to die, which no one saw flying, or offering rain, or rising up because winter had come to an end? Lower that head into just such a swamp to find out what light may have shone, what guitars, what music, how courage squandered played a keyless piano, imposture of having bested death. Drinking doubled wedding toasts, pure fear, verdicts of conscience, the strange flavor of ignorance and seeing Her before you, the one who ends it all and sways within a child in song.

For Boris / Pushkin
In memoriam

CCLXXXV

Lo que hay que decir no está dicho y flota en marismas del estruendo mundial. Ahí mesmo, abajito, donde un astro fabrica caballos del Parnaso, cavan lágrimas, guerras, dolores que fueron y se hicieron hermanos en los parajes del aujero. ¿A dónde va el fracaso de las tripas dispuestas a morir que nadie vio volar, ni dar lluvia, ni levantarse porque el invierno terminó? Húndase la cabeza en tal pantano para saber qué luz había, qué guitarras, qué música, cómo el valor desperdiciado tocó un piano sin teclas, la impostura de ganarle a la muerte. Beber dos tragos de la novia, el miedo puro, fallos de la conciencia, el extraño sabor de la ignorancia y enfrente Ella, la que todo termina y se mece en un niño que canta.

A Boris / Pushkin
In memoriam

CCLXXXVI

Mooring love to father and seafarers, erasing legacies, entering the scansion of an extinguished soul, roaming amiss in the silence he left / no discussion, premature signs, no rounds of equivocation / his tender evil, the fine fragrance of his liqueurs, his daggered silence, the pruning of one who wished to grow, ancient revolutions defeated in his black regard, the blink of his duels, kinship in a gloomy goblet, and sorrow always, always, always sorrow snuffing out the unharvested table, the helpless plates.

CCLXXXVI

Atar amor al padre y navegantes, borrar legados, entrar en la escansión del extinguido, errar en los silencios que dejó, sin argumento, sin señales precoces, sin rondas del deslizamiento, su maldad tierna, el buen olor de sus alcoholes, su silencio con dagas, los cortes al que quería crecer, viejas revoluciones derrotadas en su mirada negra, el pestañeo de sus duelos, el parentesco en copa triste, y el dolor siempre, siempre, siempre el dolor apagando la mesa sin cosecha, los platos sin ayuda.

CCLXXXVII

Unleash yourselves, furies of the hellhound, so the sky might change its color and unimaginable magnolias begin to bloom. May the patterns of worldwide anguish come tumbling down, the bloodlight that stains the balancing act of our daily bread. Every day, every plate, all the bitter servitude in obedience to the ghosts of being-here and of not. Where in years past would the carriage of humble beauty pass by? Come, with your breakage, your particles, your inner eddies, your no-sleep that caresses inexistent stars. Or hold your tongue, dead souls, far from the mercy you do not deserve.

CCLXXXVII

Desátense las furias del jodido para que el cielo cambie de color y crezcan las magnolias que nadie pudo imaginar. Que se vengan abajo los patrones de la angustia mundial, la luz de sangre que mancha las piruetas del comer. Todos los días, todos los platos, toda la amarga servidumbre obediente a los fantasmas de estar como no estarse. ¿Dónde pasaba la carroza de la humilde hermosura? Vengan con sus rajones, sus partículas, sus giros en sí mismos, su no dormir acariciando astros que no existen. O cállense ya muertos, lejos de la piedad que no merecen.

¿AND

if poetry were a forgotten memory of the dog that mauled
your blood / a false delight / a fleeting fugue in the time-worn
key of me / an invention of what can never be said? And if it
were the denial of the street / the suicide of two keen eyes /
horse manure? And if it were just some anywhere that never
sends word? And if it were?

¿Y

si la poesía fuera un olvido del perro que te mordió la sangre
/ una delicia falsa / una fuga en mí mayor / un invento de lo
que nunca se podrá decir? ¿Y si fuera la negación de la calle
/ la bosta de un caballo / el suicidio de los ojos agudos? ¿Y si
fuera lo que es un cualquier parte y nunca avisa? ¿Y si fuera?

ACKNOWLEDGMENTS

Many thanks to the editors of *Plume Poetry, Review: Literature and Arts of the Americas, Subtropics,* and the *Arkansas International,* where early versions of selections from this book were published. For their sensitive reading and keen critical input, I am once again deeply indebted to my duo of assiduous readers, Fabián Iriarte and Steve Bradbury, who help make translation a stimulating and dynamic dialogue. My sincere gratitude goes to Loorenhaus and Ledig House for granting me the uninterrupted time and inspiring spaces afforded by their priceless residencies. To my editor, Steve Halle, I must also express my appreciation for his unwavering faith in this project. My final thanks must, of course, go to the extraordinary Juan Gelman. Though he was not able to accompany me to the end of this journey, his poetry is a constant source of pleasure and wonder and inspiration.

ABOUT THE AUTHOR

Juan Gelman (1930–2014) was born of Jewish Ukrainian parents in Buenos Aires and grew up amid a myriad of languages, acquiring a fascination for words early on in life. A strange blending of social engagement and wordplay expressed in a colloquial language steeped in paradox and poignancy characterizes his poetic oeuvre, which includes more than twenty-five titles.

Having actively participated in the leftist movements that brought back Perón in 1973, he was sent to Europe in 1975 to work in public relations as a journalist. After the military coup of 1976, he lived in exile in Italy, France, Spain, and Mexico, working as a translator and journalist and denouncing human rights abuses, which also involved the personal loss as his son, Marcelo, and his pregnant daughter-in-law, who were disappeared during the dictatorship.

Gelman, considered to be one of Latin America's foremost poets, received numerous accolades during his lifetime, including the Argentine National Poetry Prize, the Juan Rulfo Prize in Latin American and Caribbean Literature, the Pablo Neruda Prize, the Queen Sofia Prize in Ibero-American Poetry, the Lateo Prize, and, the most prestigious Spanish-language literary award, the Cervantes Prize.

ABOUT THE TRANSLATOR

Born in Dayton, Ohio, **Lisa Rose Bradford** teaches Comparative Literature at the Universidad Nacional de Mar del Plata and raises horses and cattle in Madariaga, Argentina. Her doctoral work was completed at the University of California at Berkeley, and, since then, she has edited various compendiums on translation and cultural studies and three anthologies of US poetry translated into Spanish. Her poems and translations have appeared in various magazines and journals, and she has published five bilingual volumes of Juan Gelman's verse, one of which received the National Translation Award.